TRUE STORIES

THE NARRATIVE PROJECT
VOLUME I

Penchant Press International
Bellingham, Washington
U.S.A.

TRUE STORIES

THE NARRATIVE PROJECT
VOLUME I

Edited by:

Cami Ostman

Rebecca Mabanglo-Mayor

Penchant Press International
P.O. Box 1333
Blaine, WA 98231
www.penchantpressinternational.com

Publisher's Note: This is a work of memoir. Names, characters, places, and
incidents are a product of the authors' recall. Some names of individuals
have been changed. Locales and public names are sometimes used for at-
mospheric purposes. Each individual author is responsible for the content
of their work.

True Stories: The Narrative Project   Volume I

ISBN 978-0-9998048-0-3
LCCN 2018961451

Editors: Cami Ostman and Rebecca Mabanglo-Mayor
Proofreader: Andrew Shattuck McBride
Cover Photo: Lisa Dailey
Cover Design: J. Allen Fielder

Dedicated to everyone who has a story to tell.

Tears are words that need to be written.

-Paulo Coelho

The Narrative Project

A Word from the Founder:

The authors in this volume came to *The Narrative Project* with stories burning to be told. For some, they'd started their books decades ago; for others, they were still living their stories as they wrote. Our commitment to authors in *The Narrative Project*, no matter where a writer is on their journey, is to help them figure out what they really want to say and then give them everything they need to write the books they want to write.

And what is it a writer needs in order to write a book? What does it take to turn yourself into an author? Well, first of all you need to *believe that your story is meaningful and deserves to take up space* in your life and on a bookshelf one day. Maya Angelou said, "There is no greater agony than bearing an untold story inside of you." And yet, so many of us carry the burden of untold stories inside because we fear no one else will care what we have to say. Or we fear that our stories (true or fictional) will have no effect on readers even if we can find a few people willing to read the fruit of our labor. As someone who has been a psychotherapist for twenty years, I can tell you that I've never heard a story that hasn't changed my life. The idea that no one will want to read your story is simply the voice of the Inner Saboteur trying to protect you from exposure. A well-told story with the right blend of scenic detail and strongly developed theme WILL find its readers, and such a story WILL change those who spend time with it.

Many would-be authors mistake the question of whether or not the publishing industry will want their story with the question of whether or not there is an audience for it. The authors in this anthology disabused themselves of the fear that their stories were meaningless, took up the pen (so to speak), and forged through their fears. One of the first things we do in *The Narrative Project* to help people push through fear is provide *wrap around support and accountability.* Not only did each of the authors whose stories you hold in your hands now need to allow their own stories to matter, but they also had the privilege of investing in one another's stories. What you will read here represents hours of writing, critiquing, and revising. And celebrating, of course! We in *The Narrative Project* don't let writers write alone. We commit to helping each writer learn what good story-telling looks like and how to recognize it in each other's material.

But belief in one's story and support from and for others are only two of things a writer needs to complete a manuscript. As I alluded to above s/he also needs *skills.* S/he needs to know how to structure her material, how to find the story's themes, how to write dialogue, how to create characters, how to write flashbacks, how to craft scenic details, and so on. The authors in *The Narrative Project* come to us with varying skill levels. Some have taken dozens of classes and workshops in the craft of writing (indeed, some have MFAs) while others are only starting to wonder what good writing looks like. Still others have published academically and need to find their way in creative writing. Wherever a writer is at the start of our nine-month program, they are sure to grow as we talk about the specific storytelling skills they'll need to employ in order to make their stories pop off the page.

As the founder and director of *The Narrative Project,* I present this volume with profound pride and gratitude. This book represents so much commitment, support to one another, and time in skills-building and rewriting. Our coaches, administrators, editors, along with our publisher, have all worked in collaboration with the authors in this book to bring forward snippets of each writer's story that can stand alone. Look for these writers' books on the shelf of your local, independent bookstore in the future. Keep an eye out for them and be changed by their stories.

I offer a special thanks to Rebecca Mabanglo-Mayor for co-editing this anthology with me and for being a fantastic coach to our writers. To our other coaches, Wendy Welch and Colleen Haggerty, I'm grateful and feel so privileged to have you on the team. And to Anneliese Kamola, who fills in everywhere (from coach to cheerleader), thank you for sharing your giftedness and generosity with all of us!

To you, dear reader, may you be as touched by these stories as I have been. And if you're a writer, reach out to us. *We believe your story deserves to be told.*

Cami Ostman
Seattle, WA. 2018

Contents

Living Waters

By Lorinda Boyer

I've decided to not sign up for Living Waters after all, I texted The Pastor. "I think I'm just fine now. Thanks! Bye, Lorinda."

I thought that was the end of my trouble, but The Pastor called me back right away.

"Lorinda, I feel strongly that you should reconsider," he said with concern.

"You don't understand," I replied with conviction. "I have not given in for an entire week and I have no desire to. I think I'm healed."

The long, slow, seemingly exasperated exhale from The Pastor could not sway my decision. To me, there was obviously no longer a reason for me to attend the group and I was determined to prove it to him. I hung up the phone with a smile. My husband had left for work and I'd shuffled the kids off to school. Still reveling in my newfound freedom, I made my way out the back door for a run. Winding along the trail, inhaling the crisp air, I felt free.

This was how I wanted to live: carefree, unburdened by obligations to men I didn't need or want in my life. Why had I lived like a captive for so long? My pocket vibrated but I was too elated to take notice. The trail was busy and as I dodged between walkers, dogs and jogging strollers, I felt my phone vibrate again. Ignoring it again, I instead watched the trees as they swayed along the borders of the trail and listened to the crunch of the leaves under my hot pink running shoes. When I crested the first hill, I slowed at the top to gaze at the view of the city below. But when the vibrating began again, interrupting my serenity for a third time, I yanked my cell from my pocket.

Don't look at it. Just turn it off.

Unable to divert my eyes as I fumbled for the power button, I caught a glimpse of a partial message from Blake, one of those men I didn't need or want in my life.

"Have you been tested for..." the message faded.

Jamming the phone back into my pocket, I continued down the bridge. He was not going to ruin this for me. I was free now. He was in the past with the rest of them.

On the other side of the bridge, I passed a man and woman jogging together. They giggled as they chatted. She bumped playfully into his shoulder and he bumped back. Struck with a pang of irrational longing for the life I was committed to leaving behind, I wondered if they had sex in the same places along the trail as my running partner and I did—and all the other men.

Tested for what?

Fishing for my phone, I flipped it open.

"Have you been tested for STDs? For AIDS?" read the message.

Swiping at the sweat on my forehead, I read it again. A cloud covered the sun and a shiver ran through my body. Dread replaced the elation I'd felt moments before.

"No." I punched in response before zipping the phone back into my jacket pocket. Pushing the thought from my mind, I focused on my breathing and the sound of my feet hitting the ground.

There hadn't been that *many men. Why would I get tested?*

When the vibration against my ribcage became constant, I realized my phone was ringing. Fishing it out once again I pressed it to my ear, managing only a partial hello.

"How can you be sure you don't have anything?" Blake frantically cut in.

"I just *am*," I said as calmly as I could even though I *wasn't* sure.

"I want you to get tested. It's the only way I'll be able to let it go." Feeling the warmth of anger as it built in the pit of my stomach, I bit back at him.

"*You* get tested!" My hand shook with rage as I held down the power button, waiting for the screen to go dark. Turning around, my peace now completely stolen, I headed back to my house. Soon the trail gave way to the paved cul-de-sac where my house sat between two others. From there, I spotted Blake pacing back and forth in front of his black BMW parked police-barrier style across my driveway. Goosebumps popped up along my arms. Diverting my eyes from him, I ran up the stairs to my front door.

"You shouldn't be here," I mumbled as much to myself as to him. He took the steps two at a time and was right behind me as I fumbled with the front door lock.

"I'll take you to the clinic," he said, his hand closing tightly around my shoulder. My keys slipped from my hands. Trembling as I reached to pick them up, Blake gripped my shoulder. My mind flashed back to the terrifying ride from his house a week ago. The icy look in his eyes. The look he had now.

"Get. In. The. Car."

Afraid to resist and make a scene in my neighborhood, I followed him to his car.

We drove to a clinic downtown that did testing without appointments. Blake had obviously done his research. He had the exact amount of cash required and handed it over without question to the woman behind the counter. She in turn handed him a clipboard with several forms attached and a pen sprouting limp fabric daisies. With his hand in the small of my back, he directed me to a chair in the corner of the room.

"Use my address and phone number," he said after handing me the clipboard and pen, his breath hot against my cheek.

"You want the test, you fill out the papers," I said, dropping the pen and clipboard. Leaning into the chair, I rested my head against the wall as I pictured a needle the length of my arm. My stomach knotted; I hated needles.

Dressed in pink scrubs that appeared to be raining cats and dogs, a nurse approached and called out my name. Following her, I made my way down the hall away from Blake, paperwork forgotten. The nurse glanced behind us to the waiting room where he bobbed anxiously about.

"Husband?" Her glasses slid down the bridge of her nose as she peered at me over the rims. Too nervous to answer, I focused on the floor. She leaned in closer to my ear.

"Does he hurt you?"

Snapping my head up, I saw a flash of anger in her eyes.

"No," I mumbled, thankful she thought *I* was the victim.

She led me to a room and directed me to sit. My arm shook as she rolled up my sleeve, tied the heavy rubber band around it and flicked at my vein. She smiled and assured me it would be quick. Looking away, I felt a poke in my arm as she filled the tubes with my blood.

God, how had I ended up here? Hadn't I been running on the trail less than an hour ago?

Holding a cotton ball over the needle prick, I felt a rush of heat in my cheeks. The nurse said the results would come by mail to the address I'd given, though the AIDS test results could take a bit longer as they were sent out to another lab. Her words separated, landing haphazardly like alphabet magnets on a fridge door. My mind pulled at her words then attempted to arrange them into some semblance of order.

Homosexuals got AIDS. Not Christian housewives.

In the event I needed treatment, they would follow up with a phone call to the number I'd given. When I returned to the waiting room, Blake stood and reached out for my arm. Too dazed to resist, I let him guide me out of the clinic and back to his car. He opened the passenger door and waited patiently for me to settle in. Wrapping my arms tightly around my body, I felt small, empty. Feeling Blake's gaze, I turned towards him and caught a fading smile as it left his lips.

Instead of dropping me immediately back home, Blake drove us to an empty construction site we'd passed on our way to the clinic. Pulling behind an overflowing dumpster, he pushed the car into park. Still numb from the clinic experience, I closed my eyes. Blake's fingers were rough as he lifted my chin. His kiss was angry, almost cruel in its harshness. His teeth scraped along my lip leaving blood on my tongue. Opening my eyes, I saw him wipe his hand across his mouth, inspecting it. Laughing, I licked my lips and lunged at him, covering his mouth with mine. His hand went around my waist, snaked up the back of my shirt and unclasped my bra. When my breasts fell free against my bare skin, I felt the familiar rush in my chest, the ache between my legs. Blake's breath was ragged in my ear. This time he didn't shove me away when I moved down on him, then took him in my mouth. Eventually he moved above me, inside of me. Healing and freedom were not to be ours today; we were addicts, violently addicted.

When it was done, when we were done, Blake yelled at me to get dressed. Unable or unwilling to face me, he stared out the window. The sweat from my morning run had dried leaving me feeling like a human salt lick. I shook as I pulled my running clothes back on. Combing my fingers through my damp hair and pulling it into a makeshift bun, I searched around for my hat. Blake pulled it out from under his leg, tossed it in my direction. We drove back to my house in silence. Blake stared straight ahead. He swung into my driveway but didn't bother to open my door for me. I'd barely stepped back from the car when he tore down the driveway and sped off.

Crawling up the stairs to my bedroom, I pulled off my clothes once again. I stepped into the shower and turned the water up as hot as I could stand it. Steam billowed, fogging the mirrors. Letting the water run down my face, into my mouth, down my body, I hoped to burn off the smell of him. Nausea crept into my throat and I was unable to keep from vomiting. The smell made my eyes sting as I pushed the mess down the drain with my toes. Eventually the water turned cold but I remained fixed to the shower floor, frozen in my failure.

Finally, shaking and empty, I stumbled from the shower to text The Pastor.

"I sinned again," I texted. I hadn't made it more than a week without fucking-up. Without fucking. Once again, his call came quickly. His voice deep with compassion and void of judgment.

"I'll attend Living Waters," I answered my voice choked tears.

"I'll be right over to pick you up," he replied. "I'll take you to the office and help you get signed up."

Unable to catch my breath long enough to speak, I'd merely nodded into the phone.

Dread percolated in my mind the entire car ride to the church and as we parked.

"Ready?" he asked as he came around and opened my door. Dread twisted down my body and settled in my feet. Paralyzed in my fear, I remained unmoving. The Pastor, ten years older than I and classically tall, dark, and handsome, waited patiently.

"Lorinda, I know you're scared."

Understatement.

"But everything will be okay. I promise."

Taking his offered hand, I let him pull me to my feet. The church owned a couple of houses across the street from the main building. These houses were used as overflow offices for counseling, Bible Studies, and various other ministries.

Still holding tight to The Pastor's hand, I followed as he led me to a double-story blue house. It looked like any other house on the block with its neatly trimmed yard encircled by a white picket fence. The red front door framed a welcome sign painted in shapely black cursive writing.

Did anyone still write in cursive?

The sign smacked against the door as The Pastor pushed it open, shoving me gently in the direction of Deb's desk. He introduced me and I smiled, shook Deb's hand. Her grip was warm but firm.

"Nice to meet you," she said dropping a stack of paperwork into my open arms. The Pastor excused himself, saying he'd wait for me outside. My eyes followed him back out the door and he settled onto the bench we'd passed on our way in. As he leaned back, a cat jumped up and curled into his lap. How I longed to be that cat, longed to be anything, other than who I was. Deb's explanation of how important background information was, brought my attention back to the stack of papers I held in my arms. She assured the best way to know how to help me, was to know more about me.

If you knew more about me, you might not want to help me.

She handed me a pencil then directed me to a chair in a corner of the room. Sitting down, I propped my paperwork on the chair arm. A tentacle from a vine plant perched on a bookcase above wove through the open shelving, crawled down the wall, and dangled less than an inch above my head. It grabbed at wisps of my hair as if to hold me in place. Leaning away from it, I exhaled slowly.

This was a new beginning, a fresh start; I had to forget about the past. I wrote as carefully as I could. Beyond the first few, the questions were varied. Experiences, beliefs, addictions, sexual identity, nothing seemed off limits. A note at the top of the first page urged the participant to be as honest as possible.

Honest. How could a liar be honest? How could a cheater tell the truth?

"Are you currently sexually intimate with
your wife/husband? If so, how often?"

Too much. Not enough for him. There had been a time when I wanted sex with my husband. Hadn't there? It seemed a million years ago that we'd slept in the tent in his parent's yard. The ground was hard, mostly roots and rocks. It hadn't stopped us from popping a tent, covering the floor with blankets to soften the blow to our knees, our backs. When it felt as if I must surely be splitting apart, ripping in two, it stopped. He stopped. The expression on his face, in his beautiful blue eyes, was not what I'd expected. He was frightened, it seemed, by the blood he found on the blanket beneath us. In the dim light of a dying flashlight carelessly tossed aside, a faint but obvious stain. A badge for relinquishing my virginity.

After that night, sex became the end goal of every date, every interaction. We were first lovers, my future husband and me. He said he loved me. That when I was old enough, he would marry me. I assumed I must love him, too.

"Yes, infrequently," I wrote neatly in response to the question.

"Are you a survivor of child sexual abuse?"

Define survivor.

Every time my uncle pressed a quarter into my hand, brushed the hair off the back of my neck and whispered, "You're my favorite," I felt a simultaneous stab of elation at being the center of his attention and terror for the same reason. His warm breath on my shoulder, my underpants rubbing against my skin as he bounced me up and down on his knee, careful to keep my dress flared to disguise what took place beneath. Our secret. Sometimes when no one was looking, he'd grab my hand, pull me someplace to be alone. Struggling was useless since I had a small frame, little bones, no real strength to match his. His big thumbs, greedy for the velvety softness of my body would find their way inside my panties with the day of the week screen-printed across the front. Large, hot thumbs would pull my folds apart and with a gasp so loud I'd half hope, half worry he'd just died, would jam inside of me, filling the holes. Grinding against my shoulder blades as he swirled his thumbs, I'd plant my feet wide as to not end up face down on the ground. Usually quick, he'd withdraw his hands and nudge me in the back with his knee, moving me out of his way. Straightening my clothes I'd face him, waiting. He always bent down to press payment into my open palm, a debt paid to a four-year-old with no use for money.

"Yes, I am. It happened a long time ago" I scribbled in response to the question.

"Do you struggle with unwanted same-sex attraction?"

In the spirit of honesty, I should write no. It wasn't unwanted. It *should* be unwanted. Sixth grade was the first time I'd noticed my attraction to girls. A girl, Sarah Summers. Sarah was unpopular, poor and beautiful. My Christian upbringing taught me to be kind to everyone, so when Sarah and I were paired together in class to work on an art project together, we became friends. Each day when the bus pulled to a stop between the two developments, my heart would skip a beat when I spotted her. Moving my book bag into my lap, I'd pat the spot next to me and she'd flop down smelling of the morning air and toothpaste. She would envelop me in a hug and the feeling of her warm body against mine would linger in my mind all day long.

One day near the end of the school year, I asked her to come to my house. As we walked up the steep hill to my house, I was captivated by the golden strands of her hair as they lifted in the breeze.

"What do you want to do at my house?" I asked.

"Whatever," Sarah said as she shrugged and grabbed my hand. When she smiled, I felt a flutter in my stomach. We ran upstairs to my room, kicked the door shut, and flopped onto the waterbed, sending the water sloshing from one side to the other. We hung our bare feet off the edge of the bed and Sarah rested her head in the crook of my arm. We gazed up at the posters of Michael J. Fox and Ralph Macchio taped to the sparkly ceiling tiles above.

"Michael J. Fox would obviously be the better kisser," she said, turning to look at me. Her eyelashes brushed my chin sending electricity through my body. "What do you think?"

Her question got lost between her full, glossy red lips and before I could stop myself, I kissed her. Peppermint gum mixed with watermelon lip balm exploded in my mouth. Shoving me back, she slapped her hand over her lips. I willed the waterbed's tide to pull her back to me, as she struggled to sit up and bolted over the side of the bed. She grabbed for her jean jacket, scooped up her backpack, and ran out the door. Even at twelve, I knew what I'd done was unnatural, that I was a sinner. I pressed my face into the liquid filled mattress, my shame burning hot, and begged God to forgive me.

"Not really," I penciled in my answer.

Deb cleared her throat.

"There are some confidentiality forms for you to fill out," she said, "and some books to purchase when you are finished."

Nodding, I flipped through the remainder of the paperwork, relieved to find mostly yes/no questions remaining. Circling my last answer on the last page, I stood with my completed papers. Deb smiled and shoved another sheet in my direction.

"This is a release of liability. Everyone needs to sign one before beginning the program."

In the event I'm enveloped in flames upon walking through the sanctuary doors?

After scribbling my name on the dotted line, I returned the pen to Deb's desk and forced a smile.

"The first meeting is tonight in the old sanctuary," she said. "Every Monday night from six to nine o'clock p.m. for the next nine months. Bring these books." She stood, loading my empty arms once again. Nodding, I shuffled the books into the crook of one arm and headed out. As I reached for the doorknob, The Pastor jumped up, disturbing the sleepy cat, and held the door as I made my way down the steps. As I settled back into the front seat of his car, I started to cry. My mind reeled. How could I sit in a group for nine months and talk about what I'd done? And worse, what if it didn't work?

The Pastor reached over and took my hand.

"It's going to be okay, Lorinda," he said, and I wanted to believe him.

Lorinda Boyer owns and operates Belle Meadows Wellness Studio in Bellingham, Washington. She divides her time between teaching fitness classes and writing. Her upcoming memoir, *Straight Enough* is a coming-out story but more importantly, it is a coming-into story—a story of coming into an authentic life and self.

Totem Pole Journey

By Abby Brockway

I was pregnant when the Twin Towers came down. I wrapped my arms around my belly and felt a fierce love and protectiveness that pulled all my energy into keeping my baby safe from a world that was scarier than I understood.

My daughter Sienna was four months old when Master carver Jewell James of the Lummi Tribe and the other carvers working with Jewell delivered the first of a series of totem poles acknowledging the one year mark of 9/11.

The Lummi Nation, located 100 miles north of Seattle, demonstrated a quiet fierceness as they modeled what it looked like to respond spiritually to a tragedy. Lummi Carvers created a totem pole for each of the crash sites of September 11th and presented the gifts as acts of healing for the country. The first totem pole, delivered in 2002, was created for families of the victims at the site of the World Trade Center. It was 13-feet high and carved from a 140-year-old old-growth red cedar. The tree was chosen carefully, harvested because it was already struggling due to root system exposure caused by erosion.

I read and researched everything that I could about the creation of the pole, and I learned that before the tree was taken, the Lummi had a ceremony in the forest, acknowledging the tree itself, giving thanks with prayer and traditional songs that had been passed down from generation to generation by those who had stood on the same land in the same forest years ago. The endangered tree was then transformed into a new gift with a new purpose. The tree-turned-totem-pole became a peacemaker and healer as it moved across the country telling wordless stories with its symbolic colors and animal shapes.

I studied pictures of the healing totem, which showed three figures, one atop the other. At the top sat a large black-painted bald eagle. I did not know what the colors or symbols represented until I found explanations describing the carved eagle with bright yellow beak and talons shaped to represent the fathers who died at the World Trade Center. At the base was a bear with big eyes and a wide red mouth standing in for the mothers who perished on that fateful day. Nestled in the bosom of the bear was a bear cub with patterns carved and painted with red, black, yellow, and white, in remembrance of the gifts of life, liberty, and pursuit of happiness. The memory of the parents that perished during the attacks one year earlier weighed heavily on me now that I felt responsible for the four-month-old baby girl nestled at my own bosom. I learned that almost 10,000 children had lost a parent in the tragedy, and the separation between parent and child seemed unimaginable to me.

The healing pole sparked conversation and prayer as it traveled from the west coast to the east, stopping in American Indian Nations along the way for prayer and spiritual ceremony. Non-native people were also invited to participate and even to touch the totem as it traveled from town to town. It became a tangible manifestation of what it meant to begin to heal from the trauma of the 9/11 attack.

As the months marched forward, I continued to read as much as I could find about Jewell James. James shared about his personal experiences of the loss of two of his children from a car accident years ago and also began to explain the collective historical experience of grief among his people. "Native people know what grief is," James explained in an article. "We know what pain and suffering is. But we also know how to put our arms around one another." Those words entered my body. They sounded like a gospel from the mouth of a prophet. The words spelled out a truth from the other small encounters and exposure I had experienced of Native people who lived in the area around Seattle and beyond. I was drawn to the deep cultural connection that I was not able to see or feel in my own "tribe." I felt thirsty for wisdom and knowledge about how to move through life and loss—something that my culture was not easily showing me. I realized my husband Roger and I were leading

Sienna into childhood and eventually adulthood, and I needed to see how a culture and tradition could put arms around one another in times of difficulty—not with the goal of erasing pain, but to understand how to live with the brokenness and hurt that also live in and all around us.

The following year, 2003, James and the other carvers—known collectively as House of Tears—delivered an "honoring pole" to the Shanksville, PA site where United Airlines Flight 93 crashed after several passengers tried to take control of the hijacked plane. The totem depicted a bear holding a human being, alluding to the strength needed to challenge the terrorists. Sienna was now just over a year old, and though I wanted to follow the totem to Pennsylvania, I did not feel free to leave my own young family, so I stayed connected to its journey through reading, thought, and prayer.

This new totem pole was cut to a length of thirteen feet eight inches. The journey to get it to its destination lasted thirteen days, crossing 13 states in remembrance of the thirteen colonies. The last eight inches of the pole's length signified the number of delegates to the first Continental Congress established in Pennsylvania in 1774.

Three-hundred-year-old trees are hard to come by, and the western red cedar used for the 2003 totem was donated by the US forest service. This notion of the US donating the tree to the Lummi Nation I felt could be insulting, since really the trees were more in the care of the indigenous peoples for centuries before the Federal Government came along. But perhaps the sacredness of the project made the details of colonies, delegates and "donations" transcend history.

The next year I tracked a final set of totem poles as they traveled from coast to coast. The Liberty and Freedom Poles were delivered to a place near the Pentagon. The Liberty pole depicted a female bear and the Freedom pole depicted a male bear. A 34-foot "Sovereignty Crossbar" joined the two poles with eagles carved on each end and two sets of seven feathers representing American Airlines Flight 77, the plane that had crashed directly into the Pentagon. The female eagle symbolized peace, and the male symbolized war. All of the healing poles were painted red, black, white, and yellow to represent the four races that were victims of the attacks.

Jewell James was honored as an Ambassador for Peace in 2004, recognized for his tribe's efforts toward peace and reconciliation as they shared their healing traditions with the country. By this time Sienna was in preschool, and the only role in peacemaking I knew how to play, while I shuffled her back and forth every day, was to pray for her safety and for the safety of children everywhere.

Ten years later, James and The House of Tears Carvers were still sending gifts of healing to communities all over the United States for wounds to the country and to the land. James launched another totem pole journey in 2014, called, "Our Shared Responsibility–the Land, the Waters, the People." As always, I kept myself informed about the journey the totem would take.

A stop in Seattle was scheduled for August 29th. Sienna was in her tween years by then, and I was in a different place in my life. I was becoming a budding activist, ensconced in standing up for causes I believed in. I could go and participate in this ceremony! I could touch the totem pole as it passed through our community, offering a small prayer to send with the pole along its way.

I was excited to invite Sienna and Roger to join me. In the past, I had invited my family to attend environmentally-focused events, and occasionally they would agree to come because they knew it was important to me. Mid-way through an event, I would usually spot Sienna and Roger sitting on the sidelines waiting for it to be over while I enjoyed myself by connecting with those who shared common values. Maybe protests and community healing events weren't their cup of tea, but I wanted my daughter to know that we are all a part of something larger than ourselves.

It was a Friday morning when the totem pole was scheduled to stop at Saint Mark's Cathedral on Seattle's "Capitol Hill"—a beautiful summer day with temperatures in the mid 70's. Sienna was dog-sitting a small, shy Italian greyhound named E.O. Having a dog to be in charge of was an ideal job for a 12-year-old only child. Sienna would be starting school in less than a week. Dog-sitting was an opportunity for her to transition from a carefree summer to taking on some sense of responsibility. She loved to take charge, and E.O. felt comfortable with Sienna's gentle but firm leadership. I planned to take the day off to see and touch the pole at Saint Mark's Cathedral with Roger, Sienna, and E.O. in tow.

The 2014 totem pole journey of Our Shared Responsibility: the Land, the Waters and the Peoples had begun in South Dakota, moved to Montana, was passing through Washington and would go on to Canada, ending at the Beaver Lake Cree Nation, which was heavily affected by the tar sands extraction in Alberta. The long journey of the totem allowed the Lummi and affiliated tribes to share their teachings about why coal export and other fossil fuel proposals would cause harm. The trek followed the route of the coal to connect tribal nations along the coal corridor to each other. The pole's path also followed the route of the proposed tar sands pipeline, and the trek was organized to offer prayers to protect the people, water, and lands that would be damaged if the pipeline was built and broke open.

As we approached the Cathedral, a large truck with a colorful 19-foot-tall Totem Pole strapped down on its flatbed was parked in front of the Cathedral. Mother Earth was lying on her back secured with ratchet straps as she traveled from Montana's Powder River Basin, where coal is taken directly from the ground. The mother was lifting a child up. The totem also featured four warriors, representing protectors of the environment, while a green snake represented the Earth's power.

The carved green snake caught my eye. I could not wait to finally touch the totem after only reading about so many totem journeys for so many years. I felt that I myself was entering a new chapter of life and motherhood—one in which my energy was freed up from the efforts it took to care for a young child and to be replaced by new energy to expand as an activist. I was excited to meet this new phase of my life by participating in the totem pole's journey up close.

"Warrior Up" signs had been printed and were posted everywhere. More than four hundred people gathered at St. Mark's Cathedral. Sienna could not bring E.O. into the cathedral, so Roger and Sienna stayed outside while Jewell James and several other tribal leaders spoke about the journey. Several faith leaders presented a letter of apology that was originally written in 1987, the year that I graduated from high school. The letter was updated ten years later and then presented a third time ten years after that. The letter was addressed to Jewell James.

"We acknowledged the historical disrespect of traditional Native American spiritual practices and traditions. The leaders of our denominations promised to honor and defend the rights of Native Peoples ... [including] access and protection of sacred sites ... [and to] end political and economic injustice against tribal communities." The new addition addressed the new threats to the proposed terminals. The letter went on, "In this decade a new threat has arisen against Native Peoples: the mining, transport, burning, and disposal of fossil fuels. Proposed coal export terminals would damage native fisheries protected by long-standing treaties and poison our shared air and water."

The words were well-meant no doubt, but this was the third updated version of an apology that was dusted off roughly every ten years and delivered to the Lummi Tribe. It was time for some action to stand behind the words—after nearly three decades, the words fell short. I knew it, and so did most everyone in that Cathedral. With the pressures of the fossil fuel industry wanting to expand on all communities and not just native lands, suddenly many white people had woken up and realized action needed to be taken on behalf of our planet.

My heart opened. I knew I needed to listen carefully to the wisdom of the Lummi who had generations of experience defending their land and their way of life. I felt humbled to know that in my efforts to make a difference in my world, I didn't have to look far for guidance.

After the letter was read, James gave an empowered plea for us all to "Warrior Up," to not just let these words be spoken but to live into them.

I left the cathedral, walked past the totem, and ran my fingers along its base. Then I went to find my family waiting outside the Cathedral in the late summer breeze. I looked at Sienna with love. There was something I knew I needed to do— something already on my calendar that I believed could simultaneously pave the way for a better future for her while also temporarily taking me away from her. I hoped she would understand.

Two days later, I climbed eighteen feet high on a tripod and blocked an oil train from coming through my city. I was taken to jail, leaving Roger to deliver our daughter to her first day of seventh grade. For me, this is what it meant to warrior up— mother on a tripod in a railyard preventing an oil train from moving. To me, this was what fierce love looked like.

Abby Brockway is an ordinary citizen of the world. Giving birth nine months after the collapse of the Twin Towers caused her to wonder how she could participate in rebuilding the broken world, so that her daughter would inherit something good. As her daughter grew so did the words that could be used to describe Abby: troublemaker, activist, criminal, defendant, and most recent, first-time author.

Princess Sea Smoke Rows Through Choppy Waters

By Becky Burns

In the morning, my husband, Stewart, makes up a bed for me on the couch in our living room. A wedge pillow, feather pillows, and a cotton quilt open like a sleeping bag. It is a comforting place, and whether I am sitting up or slunk down, my legs can stretch out, and I can see out the window over islands, water and tree tops. Next to me, a long coffee table becomes littered with my tea mug, quart bottle, cell phone, anti-nausea meds, books, and papers. Summer streams in through the open door nearby, and I hear construction saws and hammers from the remodel across the street. I am half in my life and half out, in an in-between place.

I can't hold anything down. I grow weaker even when I try to eat and drink water. My stomach, an iron gut all of my life, has turned inside out. With my eyes closed, I hold as still as I can. As if I were on a walk along a sharp edge from which I cannot falter even a tiny bit. I steady myself. My determination keeps me on this edge; I can't teeter even an inch or I will vomit again. I open my eyes and stare into the fireplace across the room, a weak attempt to steady my vertigo.

One of the reasons I loved the house when Stewart and I bought it thirteen years ago, our first home together, was the old fireplace. When we first moved in, the fireplace hadn't been used for years. A West Coast rugged girl, I'd been given the nickname of "Princess Sea Smoke" as a young adult. Getting the fireplace to work had been a priority to me. The local chimney sweep cleaned it for us, and that night I built a fire using wood from our other property on Orcas Island. That first night, when

I'd lit the fire with one match, I'd stared into the flames and my heart had burst with warmth and memories of my youth.

Now summer keeps our fireplace quiet. As I sink into the couch, eyes closed, and let the comfort and peacefulness of home float over me, I go back to another memory of my youth— another time when home, although a very different kind of home, held me and comforted me.

Although it has been over forty years since I was 22 and living in a log cabin on a private island, my mind can enter through the threshold of that little dwelling as if it were yesterday. My island was a part of the 1000-island archipelago in the Salish Sea off the west coast of Washington State. Some of these islands are nothing but large rocks with a tussock of grass that brushes above the high tide line, while others have roads, resorts and host lots of tourists. My little island measured between three to five acres, depending on the tide and how much of the beach was exposed.

The cabin I lived in was the only building on the island. It sat smack in the middle of a grassy area and was built in the 1950s. Part of it was exposed to the westerly winds, while to the north, a sweeping madrone tree gave some shelter. On the most protected side of the cabin, I could enter Dutch doors built of planks weathered silver by the winter storms. Bits of fibrous caulking that tried to keep the weather out stuck out from between cracks in the wood. There was a latch on the door, much like a latch of a garden gate, which didn't lock. But this never bothered me, even when I left the island for days. I always simply walked out and closed the door behind me. With all of my worldly possessions inside the one room, I couldn't imagine that anyone would enter and mess with my things.

The owner of the small private island, Bill Bryant, built the cabin with his wife in the early years of their marriage. They used bleached silver cedar logs that had washed up on the beach and tumbled smooth by the rough winter waves. The logs had been brought ashore with a Come-Along and stacked on top of each other to make the walls. In the 1950s, no federal official had thought of building permits, wrought with limitations of creativity, so the cabin was not square and not level, but it suited me fine. Bill and his wife had moved a short rowboat ride away on Orcas Island.

In the winter of 1972, I met with Bill to come up with the arrangement for renting the island. After a failed attempt at college, I longed for solitude. Since I'd grown up on Orcas, I knew these islands. I knew this cabin had been built with love and was laced with dreams of a happy place to get away from it all. That's what I needed. After considering my financial situation, I informed Bill I could afford to pay him forty dollars a month. We talked for quite some time, he told me that he needed a caretaker for his island and he would pay me forty dollars a month to watch over things. We parted company that day, both feeling as if we had gotten the better end of the deal.

One late summer afternoon, wearing torn jeans and my favorite blue checkered shirt, I wandered down to a sandy spit. I knelt on a bed of crushed shell and chunked out blocks of sand with my shovel through the wet debris. Sometimes I used an oversized clam shell to scoop and dig, but that day I pulled manila clams out of the ground one by one with a proper shovel. I tossed them each with a clunk into my steel bucket until I had a mound of white nuggets, plenty for my meal for one.

Back at the cabin, I pushed the door open. The bright sunlight trickled into the dark single room—my sixteen-by-sixteen foot womb. I stepped inside. The door made a soft, mossy thump when it shut behind me. Two beds, built with end-to-end thick boards, lay along one side of the cabin. The ceiling was made of rough-hewn rafters with split cedar shakes that lent a golden hue to the whole space, and thick weathered planks, one foot wide and rounded at the sides, ran the length of the floor. It was always difficult to sweep the floor clean; all the bits of life fell into the grooves between the imperfect wood. As I moved across the floor with my bucket, the boards rocked underfoot and creaked stories of days gone by. Right inside the door was a small ship's stove. Black cast iron with porcelain knobs and an oven barely big enough to hold a nine-by-nine inch pan. Most of my meals cooked on the stove came from the sea. One of my favorite shellfish was the butter clams I carried in the bucket. I planned to steam them in an oval aluminum pot and to savor every morsel.

The next morning, I was back in the summer sunshine, but this time, I threw a crab pot off my rowboat and returned in the evening to pull it up and find that it was filled with thirty Dungeness crabs. A thrill filled me at the idea of the steam from the boiling water on the stove cooking those crabs. I would eat them day after day, but I knew I had too many to eat myself, so I put several of the scampering live crabs in the bottom of my rowboat and took them for a ride to Orcas Island. There were expensive yachts tied up from Canada at the yacht club dock in Westsound that day.

I pulled alongside the float in my worn down rowboat. "Anyone wanna buy fresh crab I just caught? One crab for a dollar," I called out. I knew a dollar was probably too low a price, but there was nothing to buy back on my island anyway.

I shipped my oars and they balanced in the middle seat. Well-dressed yachters emerged from their boats with buckets. Squatting next to my skiff, I gingerly plucked the crabs as they ran for their lives over the backs of their friends. I was a pro at not getting pinched and knew just how to grasp them as I flung the crustaceans into the buckets.

Later, rowing back to my island with a pocket full of dollars, I realized besides solving the problem of too many crabs to eat, I had never been so rich!

The size of the cabin was perfect for me. I was grateful it wasn't any larger in that there was no electricity on the island. My heat source was a Franklin fireplace. Efficiency was sacrificed for the charm of an open fire that faded at the end of an evening. After selling the crabs and returning with just enough for my own needs, I lit the fire and sat in a comfy wicker chair covered with a sheepskin that filled in the crannies of the wicker and matted to my shape. I never tired of staring into the fire. On wintery mornings, I would wake up to icy crystals on the insides of the small paned windows and would run across the floor in my bare feet to build a fire as quickly as possible before running back to my bed piled high with thick quilts to wait for the flames to thaw out the freezing morning chill. But that night after selling the crabs, the Northwest summer was warm enough that the fire served mostly as company instead of savior.

Next to the fireplace was a hand water pump which fed off an outside cistern that held a collection of rainwater from the roof. When I was ready to finish my chores for the evening, I got up from my happy reflections next to the fire and pushed on the handle. The water sputtered and pulsated into a shallow white enamel bowl. I used the water to rinse my face and to wash the dishes. During the years I lived in my cabin, I'd devised a system for cleaning my dishes. After heating up soapy water on the stove, I collected a bin of salt water as my rinse water. After scrubbing the dishes in the soapy fresh water, I dipped them in the rinse water, leaving behind a salty film. Ready for my next meal; perfectly salted!

Then it was time for bed. From the window next to my bed, I drifted off to the muffled sound of lapping water on the gravel beach below the cabin. Such sweetness.

Living on the island taught me about self-sufficiency. I hauled logs from the beach and chain-sawed them into sizes that I chopped for firewood. I cleaned the chimneys of my kerosene lanterns and trimmed the wicks, and then I used one match to light up my golden night world. I ate from the sea and lived according to the tides. I had a life made by hand in every way.

Over the years in the 1970s that I lived on Sheep Island, the locals called my island "Becky's Island." It was one of a handful of small islands off the west coast of Orcas Island. In the 1850s, Lummi Indians had settled in the area and found the beaches of Westsound provided an abundance of clams. In the summers, the warlike First Nations Haida Indians came down in canoes from British Columbia and killed the Lummi natives. My island became a sacred burial ground for these people. I knew where the Lummi bones were on my island. Over the years, the winter storms eroded the soil and laid bare their stories. The bones were woven amongst the roots of the trees on the beach where I read away my summer days. There was a burial site in the middle of the island where the top of a cranium was exposed. An Orcas old-timer told me once that a typical burial meant the body was placed in a hole in a seated position with the head at the top, to enable the spirit to enter and exit. I walked by these burial sites every day on my way to the beach, my garden, and to the outhouse. Some people would have gotten the creeps living on a small island alone with these bodies. For me, I felt protected by ancient people. Together we lived in peace.

Now, so many years later, when my own bones are tired and my own body is fighting for life, I gaze at the fireplace in a different house. Not a cabin—a big, beautiful, welcoming home in a small city full of live people. We don't need to heat this house in the summer, so the fireplace is just an opening with the potential for a vibrant winter blaze.

Stewart is in the next room. Alone, I reflect on how I have lived with spirits of the Natives all of my life. I was fortunate to grow up on Native land that has since been passed down to me from four generations of my family. Guided by these Natives, I became drawn to the spirit world. Years after leaving the cabin, I became a hospice volunteer and helped people who were dying as they moved each day closer to death. I cooked for them, cleaned their homes, sat and held their hands at their bedside, and sang to them as my voice cradled them to sleep. I learned to leave my life at the threshold as I entered a dying person's world. I became a vessel of comfort, giving each person whatever they needed for time left in this world. I learned to say good-bye each day as I left their homes, holding their gaze an extra second longer, saying another silent good-bye in my heart as I walked out the door.

Walking away from these dying people often reminded me of walking out of the cabin one winter night when the moon called to me and I knew I had to be on the water. That night a thick-bladed screwdriver clanked in the bottom of my metal bucket. In my other hand, a flashlight danced light and shadow. On the steep gangplank, I held onto the railing as my boots slid from rung to rung. Across the frosty float I stepped gingerly until I stood alongside my rowboat. With my gloved hand, I wiped off the mixture of rain and condensation from the middle seat of my boat. I untied the bow line, then the stern line. Keeping my center of gravity low, I swung myself into my boat with a slow easy motion. I pushed off from the float, planted the oars into the oarlocks and began steadily pulling away from the island. That night, my destination was Skull Island, to harvest oysters.

I rowed to the unheard harmony between wood and sea. Despite the layers of bundled clothes, I was as graceful as a dancer. I remembered myself as a young girl in my leotard and fabric shoes. I struggled for a year to perfect one simple step. Leap, toe, flat! The European teacher wielded a cane that struck the floor near my awkward feet. My mother stood nearby, with a disapproving look on her face. I was failing at her effort to make me into a dancer, a young cultured lady. The ballet lessons were the first in a line of attempts to force me into the spirit of someone I wasn't: etiquette classes, how to walk in a straight line with a book on my head like a lady, how to sit properly, how to speak distinctly. These classes all accumulated into the grand event of my coming out as a debutante when I turned eighteen. The Debutante Ball, held at the Sunset Club in Seattle in 1968, was where I curtsied my way into society in front of the seated matriarchy wearing a white long gown, hiding behind a dozen red roses, laughing with my friends as I felt out of my element.

All of my life, in my rowboat, I have been in my element. The toes of my boots pushed against the plywood seat in the stern. My hands grasped the cold dripping oars and I pulled with a languid force. My body rose and fell, dipped and swayed. Silky smooth, the bow of the boat parted the water like a zippered seam.

I rowed like I moved through my life. I pulled on the oars, using every muscle, my entire body engaged. I threw my body into the rowing, as I now throw myself into my life. All in, never partial. After every deep pull on the oars, I paused and filled my chest with breath.

Now, forty years after leaving my island, I know that sometimes the water is choppy, so I pull harder and lean further into my desire to move forward, to live. Today, sitting in my living room, cancer is my choppy seas. My stomach tosses me around, and tries to throw me out of the boat of my body. I call on the spirits of the Natives that have guided me throughout my life. With their help, I know I will get through this turmoil with determination and grace and one stroke at a time.

Becky Burns feels that she was blessed to grow up every summer in a remote part of Orcas Island. Always following her own path, as a single mother, she founded the company Anahola Granola on Kauai. She is a lover of islands, an entrepreneur, and a doting grandmother. She writes stories that highlight the beauty of human relationships and show us all how resilient we are capable of being.

SUSIE VOTES

By Anne Ciochetto

S usie awoke to the baby whimpering in the next room and
immediately eased herself out of bed, being careful not to
disturb Andrew. She grabbed her worn chenille robe as
she left the chilly room and waited until she had gently closed
the bedroom door before slipping it on. A faint glow from the
kitchen's oil lamp provided enough light to guide her steps. She
knew that her oldest, Delbert, was already up and likely to be
hard at work milking the cows and beginning the day's farm
chores. A mother could not have asked for a better son. She
thanked God every day for bringing him into the world first.
His kind heart and steady support were blessings beyond
measure. She knew that he was the one she could always count
on and that meant a lot during these hard times.

As she padded down the hall, she could hear Esther moving about in her crib, her whimper on the verge of a full cry.
When she entered the room, Esther looked up with her big dark
eyes and held her arms out. Susie bent down, gathered her
youngest in her arms, and exited before the other children
awoke.

After a quick change and feeding, she tucked Esther and
her ragdoll into a makeshift bed on the kitchen floor and proceeded with her morning routine. First, she had to get the old
wood stove going. She smiled when she saw that Delbert had
the stove ready for her. Susie struck a match and held it until
the newspapers captured the flame, then watched as the kin-
dling also caught fire. Once she was sure the stove was warming, she went to the icebox and retrieved the pans of cornmeal

mush she'd prepared the night before. Her eyes glanced at the clock—5:30—plenty of time before she had to leave.

Susie ran a knife around the edge of each loaf pan, inverted them onto the wooden cutting board, and sliced each loaf into eighths. While lard heated in the old iron skillet, she grabbed a small saucepan and mixed a simple syrup of sugar and water. Then, because today was special, she added a few tablespoons of Mrs. Dedrick's apple butter, infusing the syrup with the richness of a fall harvest, and bringing the comforting aroma of cinnamon into the kitchen.

While the golden slices of mush were slowly turning a delicate brown, Susie pondered the day ahead. Tuesday, November 8, 1932, Election Day. There had been a lot of excitement and controversy leading up to this election. Even now, a few hours before she would cast her vote, she was still torn between the two major candidates.

This was the fourth time she'd voted for President since women gained their rights in 1920. She took elections seriously and until recently thought she'd been doing the right thing for her family and for her country. Her first vote was for Warren Harding who promised a "return to normalcy" after the horrors of World War I. Life for her family had been good under President Harding, although it was a shock when he died of a heart attack before the end of his term. Then Vice President Coolidge stepped in and she even voted for him when he ran for president on his own. There was nothing flashy about him and she liked that. His thoughtful, deliberate approach, "Safe, Sane, Steady," was what people like her wanted and needed, especially after the uncertainty of the war years. In the last election Herbert Hoover had promised a new period of prosperity, "a chicken in every pot and a car in every garage." She'd voted for him but regretted it just seven months later when the stock market crashed and started the country on a downhill slide toward the worst times she'd ever known.

Now here they were, into the third year of the Depression and barely making it after the grasshopper invasion last summer destroyed most of the crops. Her husband Andrew and her older boys found occasional jobs with the county, clearing snow or helping with park and road maintenance, but the jobs were scarce. They scraped by on what the boys could get from hunting or fishing and what she could grow in her small vegetable garden. Occasionally, when things were really bad, the county provided a few groceries. It was embarrassing that once again today she'd have to send her children to school with a lunch of cold biscuits and lard. The past few years had been such a struggle. Something just had to change!

She flipped four slices of mush and wondered how Hoover could use the slogan "We are Turning the Corner." He should visit Hadley, Minnesota, or any other place in Murray County and then he'd know that no one was turning the corner, unless it was the corner into losing their farms, their jobs, and their businesses.

The sweet aroma of breakfast wafting down the hallway was enough to get the younger children out of bed. They came streaming into the kitchen, rubbing their eyes and yawning.

"I'm hungry," whined Harvey.

"Sit down, your breakfast is ready," Susie replied. Harvey was always hungry lately. He'd be six next month and she figured he was probably due for a growth spurt.

"I made some special syrup for you this morning. I think you'll like it," she said as she spooned the apple butter concoction over the browned mush slices.

"Fried mush, my favorite," said Harold, age nine, sitting down next to Harvey. "Can I have two slices, Ma?"

"There's enough for everyone to have two slices," she replied, "but no more than that."

The kitchen went silent again as the children devoured their meal. Susie continued cooking since Andrew and the older children wouldn't be far behind.

Once the young'uns finished, Susie shooed them down the hall. "You all get into the bathroom and wash up now. You'll need to leave for school in about thirty minutes and be sure to wear something warm, the wind is starting to kick up. We could be in for a storm later on."

In the early morning light, Susie had noticed clouds moving in. While the children were eating, the sun broke through briefly in pale yellow and dusty pink, then just as quickly darkened again. Fall, her favorite season, had had a long run this year but she knew that winter would soon make its appearance. The morning air carried with it the feel of a coming snow.

Her thoughts returned to the election quandary. Could she vote for the Republican Hoover again? He'd already had three years and it had only gone from bad to worse. Or should she take a chance and vote for Franklin Roosevelt whose promise of "Happy Days are Here Again" might only be an empty platitude? Her thoughts wrestled with each other even while she served Andrew and the boys, who'd come in from their chores. Removing the last of the fried mush from the skillet, she knew what she had to do.

After the younger children left for school, Susie finished her own quick breakfast and took a few minutes to quickly put herself together. While Esther played with her ragdoll on the bathroom floor, Susie washed up and combed out her thin, dark blond hair. She fashioned two long braids and wrapped them around her head, pinning each braid securely in several places so she wouldn't have to worry about it for the rest of the day. Then she walked back to the bedroom and exchanged her nightdress and robe for a slip and one of her cotton dresses. Today she chose the one she'd made most recently, a cheerful blue and yellow calico print with sapphire blue buttons and a matching belt. The colors brought out her blue eyes and she felt her spirits lift as she guided the dress over her head. After getting into a pair of heavy cotton stockings, she slipped on sensible black oxfords and tied each one in a double knot. Esther was at the age where she liked to pull at the laces thinking it was a game, and Susie sure didn't want to spend all day retying her shoes.

She picked the baby up and walked back to the kitchen where Andrew sat with the three older boys lingering over cups of watered-down coffee.

"I'm going in to town to vote," she announced. "I need you to keep an eye on Esther."

"Sure. We ain't got nothin' better to do with our time," muttered Andrew.

"Who are you voting for, Ma?" asked Robert, her second oldest.

"You know we don't discuss that," Susie said sternly. "There is a reason they call it a secret ballot. It's so people can vote freely and not have to worry about what other people think."

"Alright, Ma. I was just wondering. If I could vote, I'd tell you. Me and my friends all think that Roosevelt is the man for the job. You know, 'Happy Days are here again...' " Robert burst into song as he often did, trying to lighten things up.

"Well, you and your friends aren't voting, I am," said Susie, "and maybe we'll have *Happy Days*, and maybe we won't. We'll have to see."

At the front door she stopped to put on a scarf and coat, picked up her pocketbook, and looked around to be sure she wasn't missing anything.

"Now you be a good girl," she called out to Esther. The front door creaked as she stepped into the crisp November breeze.

Susie walked a few steps away from the farmhouse, then stopped for a moment and looked up at the mottled sky and around at the bare fields with just a few dried cornstalks remaining here and there. She took a deep breath in and felt the change. She was ready for a snowy blanket to cover the summer's devastation, to erase some of the memory of what had happened. She was ready for the quiet stillness, the hush that seemed to bring a restful comfort to the land. Yes, she was ready for a change. But first she had to vote!

She set out again with purpose, heading down the dusty country road into town. Her firm footsteps took her up and down the low hills that lay between the farm and Hadley. She smiled to herself as she thought about the children and how they thought the hills were mountains. She had grown up in the Mountain State – the children would be astounded if they could see a real mountain. Continuing on, she counted the rising and the falling of the road – five "mountains" would take her to the lake just outside of town, and then it was a short distance down Main Street to the town hall.

It took about forty-five minutes, although she'd been so lost in thought, it seemed much shorter. As she walked into the center of town, she stopped to admire the last vestige of color on the tree-lined street. November was her favorite month with the changing colors and crackling of leaves underfoot. But now the breeze was getting stronger, blowing the leaves about her ankles. With her pocketbook dangling from her elbow, she reached up with one hand to pull her scarf tighter to her chin and gathered her coat closer with her other hand. Continuing on for another block, she approached the town hall, climbed the wooden stairs, and entered the building, grateful for the comforting warmth within.

Susie proceeded to the voting area where the election official located her name in a large leather-bound book. After signing in, she took her ballot and waited for an open booth. Despite the early hour, there was already a longer-than-usual line. The room was enveloped in a deep, echoing hush, broken only by an occasional whisper or a stifled cough. As people came in, she could hear the tapping of shoes on the wooden floor and pages rustling as the election official searched through his book. Otherwise, each person was silent, the weight and seriousness of their responsibility creating an aura of deepest respect.

Susie played her decision over and over during the half-hour wait. When it was her turn, she stepped forward to the voting booth and pulled the black curtain behind her. Alone with the ballot, she scanned six pairs of names, her choices for President and Vice-President of the United States. At the top, Democratic candidates Franklin Delano Roosevelt and John Nance Garner. The Prohibition candidates were next followed by the Republican incumbents, Herbert Hoover and Charles Curtis. She hesitated. For as long as she could remember, her folk had embraced independence and self-sufficiency and rejected government interference. Now those things she held so dear were being forced from her. Hoover stood fast with his philosophy of "rugged individualism" and minimal government intervention, something her family had believed in since the American Revolution. But during the past three years, his policies had sunk the country deeper into economic hardship, and there was no end in sight. How could she possibly vote for him?
Susie scanned the last four names, a Socialist, a Communist, and representatives from the Socialist Labor and Liberty parties. None of those fit with her beliefs. She really had only one choice. It felt like a betrayal of all she had ever believed in but this time she had to think of what was best for her eight

children. Mr. Roosevelt promised a "New Deal" of government programs that would help with jobs, restore the economy, and get people back on their feet again. He was their only chance.

She looked down at her ballot, read the instructions and with steady hand and firm resolve marked a clear black "X" in the first box. After voting for the local offices and issues, she inhaled deeply, put the ballot in its plain envelope, picked up her pocketbook, and left the booth, sending a silent prayer up to God. As she deposited the envelope into the locked metal box on the clerk's table, she heard the softness of paper falling on paper - her vote joining with many others in the quiet sound of democracy.

Susie walked toward the exit, her heels making a loud *thunk-thunk, thunk-thunk* against the room's silent hush. Self-conscious, she slowed her steps and tried to walk toe-to-heel to lessen the noise. Approaching the door, she felt a tap on her elbow and turned to see her friend, Mary Stolle. She smiled and they left the building together.

Outside and free to speak, Susie remarked, "I believe the temperature dropped at least ten degrees while we were inside."

Mary looked up at the darkening sky.

"The sky's gotten more depressing, too," she said. "And the wind is picking up. I think we're finally in for a visit from Old Man Winter."

"You could be right," replied Susie. The two women locked arms, braced themselves against the wind, and walked back down the street.

"John has the wagon down at the General Store," said Mary. "We can give you a ride partway home if you'd like."

"I'd be most grateful," Susie replied. "By the looks of things the weather isn't going to be getting any better." The two friends continued to chat as they walked down the street, bringing each other up-to-date on their children and their school projects, discussing what needed to still be done to get ready for winter, and commiserating about the effects of the drought and grasshoppers on the crops this past season. Their small talk felt safe and hid the anxiety and hopes for the future that Susie knew both she and Mary felt about this Election Day.

The Stolles took her two-thirds of the way home before they turned off toward their own farm. Shortly after they left her, a fine mist began to fall and by the time Susie reached the turnoff for her farm, a few light snowflakes began to appear.

She walked through the front door and found Andrew dressed and sitting on the sofa, turning his hat in his hands. He hadn't felt well that morning and said her vote could count for the two of them, but now he seemed better and anxious to cast his own vote. Before she said anything, he stood up, put his hat on, and then reached down to baby Esther who was sitting on the floor. He patted her on the head.

"I'll be back soon, princess. You be good for your Ma," he said, then he turned to Susie. "The weather looks like it's taking a turn for the worse. I'll take the horse into town just to be on the safe side."

Andrew returned an hour later covered with white flakes. In that short time the rain had changed to snow. By early afternoon, the younger children were back from school.

"They sent us home early," each cried out as they entered the back door into the kitchen.

"Teacher says there's a big storm coming," said Harold. "He said something about Old King Boreas visiting us."

"Oh, really?" said Susie.

"Yes, King Boreas is the god of the wind, and he's going to swoop down and bring winter to Minnesota. And, and," he said breathlessly, "his daughter comes with him and brings the snow!"

"That's quite a story," said Susie, smiling at Harold's young face, his wide blue eyes showing that he was thoroughly convinced of his new truth.

Throughout the afternoon the family watched the snow coming down thicker and faster. The wind gained strength, whistling around the corners of the house, and rattling the walls until everyone inside wondered if the house was strong enough to remain standing. Gale force gusts blew snow into drifts and plastered the sides of buildings with a fine white powder. The blizzard raged with such fury throughout the day that not one of the children even gave a thought to going outside. Instead, they gathered in the living room, wrapped in Susie's handmade quilts, and took turns being closest to the fire. After a simple supper featuring pheasants the older boys had brought home from their hunting trip the day before, the family retired to wait out the storm.

Wednesday came and went with the blizzard continuing on until late afternoon. The children were stuck inside, happy to miss school, and Harold regaled the younger children with stories, each more fantastic than the one before. Susie was grateful for the imagination and creativity that kept them entertained. Meanwhile she and her oldest daughter Lillian spent the day in the basement digging out the family's winter clothing, determining which clothes fit each child, and making a list of items still needed to fill in the gaps. She longed for the day when she'd be able to provide new clothing and winter boots for each of them, but knew that this year they'd have to once again make do with what they had and what they could find at the church's clothing shelf.

Thursday dawned clear and calm. Susie went through her morning admiring the bright blue sky, broken here and there by soft wispy clouds. In less than 48 hours, the entire landscape had changed. The drifts, almost like sculptures, sparkled in the sun as if tiny diamonds had been strewn across the fallen snow. Fall leaves no longer graced the few trees around the house. Instead, they stood as barren grey figures against a blanket of snow. For Susie, this transformation could not have been more breathtaking.

While preparing breakfast her thoughts turned to the election and she wondered what the result had been. She didn't have to wait long to find out. Delbert had been out early helping Mr. Dedrick clear the road between their houses and he'd come running back in with the Dedricks' newspaper to report that Roosevelt had won by a landslide, 42 states for Roosevelt and only six for Hoover.

Later that day, while Esther was down for a nap, and the rest of the family were out shaking off cabin fever, Susie sat down with a cup of tea and read about the election in the paper. When the ballots across the country were counted, Roosevelt and Garner had won with 89% of the electoral vote. For a moment she allowed herself to daydream about what these changes would mean for her family. At the top of her list was steady work for Andrew and the older boys, and then, maybe one day, a home of their own, one that would always be warm and comfortable, and where they wouldn't have to worry about constantly moving.

And then she thought about the little things that would mean a lot to her children. She saw them walking to school with full lunch pails that included meat or cheese, some fresh fruit and occasional treats. And she imagined how much better they would feel being able to buy their own new workbooks instead of making do with used ones. She pictured herself placing a dime in their small, outstretched hands so that they could attend a school performance or take in a picture show. And she thought about how different winter would be if they all had warm coats and if their rain shoes could be replaced with real snow boots. She didn't want much for herself, but she did want a better future for each of her children.

As she took another sip of tea, she glanced down at the paper. President Roosevelt's inauguration day seemed so far off—March 4, 1933—another four months. Well, she thought, change might be coming, but it wouldn't be soon. There was at least one more hard winter ahead of them. She folded the newspaper and said a silent prayer for her children and for a future that might be filled with Happy Days once again.

Anne Ciochetto is a historian and genealogist whose passion is recreating past times in vivid historical detail. Anne has been a contributor to *The Minnesota Genealogist* and to *Follow Me Back in Time* by Joan Ellis. Her forthcoming nonfiction novel, *From Prairie Skies to Coral Seas,* follows a Minnesota family through the Depression, the CCCs, and the Pacific war.

In the Red Kitchen

By Barbara Clarke

Normandy, Missouri 1948

I didn't know turning six last year could be so hard. First, I had my tonsils out in the hospital. Then, not long after that, Mom dreamed that I fell through the open kitchen door and down the basement steps. She hugged me when I appeared alive the next morning and told me her bad dream. When I asked her if I died she held me tighter. I guess I did.

Then, my parents had a trial separation. Mom took me and my older brother Bud, who was in sixth grade, to live with her parents, Grandma Rosie and Grandpa John Klumb. Dad had to drive across town to pick us up at our elementary school. He looked sad and Mom cried when I asked her if we could go home. I missed our dog, our house, and having two parents under the same roof. At the end of the week they said that they had decided to try again. We moved home and whenever they argued, I wondered if we would have to move back to Grandma Rosie's house or worse, that they would get a divorce.

And then, in August Mom surprised us. I'd been at my friend Jane's house. Her mom took us swimming at the Ferguson Pool for most of the day, and I'd just gotten home. Mom wouldn't let me in the kitchen. At five on the dot, I waited outside on the front steps for Dad to come home from work. He had his suit coat slung over his shoulder and his tie pulled down as he walked up our sidewalk.

"This is the hottest July I can remember," Dad said and sat down on the steps with me. "Lucky you, you got to go for a swim today."

"It was fun, but do you know about Mom's surprise? She has a sheet over the kitchen door and a Keep Out sign pinned on it."

"No idea, kiddo. But if we go in and get off these hot concrete steps, we might find out."

We could smell paint coming from the kitchen but waited for Mom to call us in. My older brother Bud joined us.

"Okay, you three, dinner's ready." She pulled the sheet aside, stepped through, and revealed the mystery.

"Oh," we said in unison.

"Chinese red," she said, directing our surprised faces to each of the freshly-painted walls. She gestured like the lady on TV who sold refrigerators. Dad, Bud, and I surveyed the glossy walls from the doorway. I waited for Dad to say something, but his mouth opened and then closed, like he wanted to think first.

"Well," Mom said, "just don't stand there gawking, come in and let's eat. I didn't have time to make a fancy meal. Bunny, don't touch that wall since the paint isn't completely dry."

I wouldn't dare touch it.

"It sure is red," Bud said. He pulled his chair out from the red Formica table and sat down. My mother looked expectantly toward my father.

"You hate it."

"Hate's a strong word for paint," Dad said. "I'd like to decide for myself."

He joined Bud and sat down. Bud was in a bad mood, and when I tried to squeeze past him to get to my place, he jutted his chair back, knocking me into the basement door. Thankfully, last year after Mom had her bad dream Dad screwed a big hook and eye on the top to make sure it stayed closed.

The kitchen felt hotter now that it was red. I looked at the hamburger patty on my plate. Ever since the babysitter told me where meat came from, the thought of a poor cow having to die for my supper bothered me. I thought of blood and felt queasy, but sat down at the table and decided I could start with the lime Jell-O salad and then try the green beans next to the meat.

"I like it, Mom." I tried to sound pleased. Bud pretended to drop his red and white checkered napkin on the floor and leaned over.

"Liar," he said and pinged my leg with his fork.

"Something wrong with your dinner?" Mom asked. I shrugged and ate a few green beans.

The small fan that sat on the counter sent a wimpy breeze around the room as it swiveled back and forth. The big red skillet on the stove was only a few feet away from us and every time the breeze came toward me I could smell the grease of the hamburger.

"You better get busy there," Dad said, nodding at me and then toward the street beyond the kitchen window where we could hear the neighborhood kids beginning to gather. I finished my glass of milk.

"So, this is what you were up to today," Dad said, gesturing with his empty fork around the room.

"I can tell you don't like it," Mom said. "It's a lot cheaper than wallpaper and this room needed something besides all white walls, tiles, and cabinets. It's the latest style and, anyway, it's done."

Bud finished his dinner and faced me with his mouth open, showing me a last wad of half-chewed hamburger.

"See you, slowpoke," he said, sending a spit spray my way. He pushed his chair back, dashed through the house, and let the screen door bang behind him.

"So, did you have a good time last night?" Mom asked while she refilled Dad's iced tea glass. I looked over at Dad, waiting for his answer.

Oh, no. I saw a pillow and blanket folded up on the couch when I came through the living room this morning. This conversation wasn't going anywhere good.

"It was fine," Dad said. He didn't look up, pulled the sports section of the newspaper up from under his chair, and started reading. The air felt electric. Something besides the heat and the red paint was going on between my parents. I could tell a fight was brewing by the way my mother kept staring at my father who was acting like he didn't notice. I wished I could jump up and dash out the door like Bud.

"Where did you get the idea, Mom?" Maybe if I asked about the kitchen Mom wouldn't ask about Dad coming home late last night.

"Marge and I saw a red kitchen in her women's magazine."

"I've never heard of a red kitchen," my father said looking up from the paper.

"Well, Dorsey, now you have." Mom pressed her lips together like she was keeping bad words in. She pushed her chair back, went over to the sink, and made louder than usual noises starting the dishes.

"Are you having your stomach troubles again?" Mom asked me as she cleared more from the table.

"I'm just not hungry. It's too hot."

"Then go . . . wait, at least finish your beans." I picked up my fork, but before I could stab a few, she leaned over and swooped up my plate.

By the time I joined the kids outside playing hide and seek it was dusk, and sheet lightning was flashing above our neighborhood. I ran down the front steps and squeezed into one of my favorite hiding places between the prickly spirea bushes and the wall directly under our kitchen window. I could hear my mother at the sink, turning the water faucet on and off. My father must have been pacing like when he was angry, his voice faded and then came back loud enough for me to hear.

"You have no idea what we did." His words came out slowly, one at a time, like talking to Grandpa John who can't hear that well. "I told you. A group of us met after work for a drink. Only Sylvia and I wanted to go to the early show. We got a bite to eat afterward and I was home by midnight. It was damned innocent if you ask me. Besides, I'm entitled to an evening out now and then. Why get so mad about nothing?"

"Nothing! I work my butt off around here."

I pictured Mom's brown eyes flashing.

"Damn you. I'll tell you who's entitled. I am. It sounds like a date to me. You get an evening out while I'm stuck here with the kids."

Flashes of lightning and thunder claps came closer bringing the first bit of a cool breeze that stirred the bushes.

"Your pal Sylvia. She's a married woman who acts like a bitch in heat so don't flatter yourself."

"You know nothing about her. You're the one being the bitch, Em."

My chest was so tight, I could hardly breathe. This was the worst fight since we'd stayed at Grandma Rosie's house.

I'll go in and say I need a drink of water and maybe they'll stop.

I left my hiding place, dashed up the front steps, tiptoed through the darkened living room and stopped at the kitchen doorway, partially hidden by the sheet still hanging from one tack. The only light on was over the sink. I didn't feel very brave and wished Bud were home. Dad said something I couldn't hear and then he stepped back from the sink. Behind the sheet in the dark hallway I couldn't see him for a second.

"You bastard." Mom spiraled away from the sink toward Dad, water drops flying off her fingers. She landed her whole body on him, slamming him against the refrigerator, like a wrestler on TV. Mom was on her toes, stretched to Dad's height, standing firm against him. His breath came out in one long "Ooomph." They looked so odd, like they were going to dance. But, then I saw something in my mother's hand glisten in the light. It was a kitchen paring knife, and it was poised at my father's neck, the point making a triangle in his pale skin. I blinked hard to be sure.

Hurry, get in there . . . but I couldn't move my feet. They both went silent. My father's eyes were wide, staring at the red wall. I heard the clock tick off the seconds, or was it my heart?

"Be careful . . . think about what you're doing." Dad barely moved his mouth. His shoulder was tilted downward under my mother's grip. The knife was still poking into his neck.

Go—but what if I surprised her and the knife goes in? Who could I call for help? I took a step into the kitchen doorway just as my mother's shoulders gave way, like letting air go out of a balloon. I held on to the doorframe to keep from buckling. *"Please. Mom and Dad,"* but no sound came out.

My father continued looking at the red wall across from him and then his eyes shifted over to the doorway where he saw me.

"There now," he said, gently lowering her arm. He eased Mom back, opened her hand, and slowly took the knife. My mother reached behind her for a chair and collapsed onto it. Her sobs escaped her and filled the silence. When she dropped her head her wavy brown hair hid her face; her fists clenched on her lap.

Dad opened the metal drawer at the end of the counter and put the black handled knife in the section where it belonged.

"Don't ever do that again . . . unless you think you can finish the job," Dad said over Mom's sobbing. Then he walked through the doorway, tripped over the red-paint-spattered sheet on the floor, and collided with me. "For Christ's sake, Bunny. Go outside with the other kids."

His rough shove sent me running through the house, down the steps, and into the front yard. I slipped back into my place behind the bushes and waited for my heart to stop banging in my ears. What if Dad hadn't seen me? Maybe I saved his life? What if Mom had stabbed him? Where would Bud and I go when the police took her away? The worst pictures zinged through my head. I put my hands on both sides of my face, shut my eyes, and asked my brain to please be quiet. I hated that red kitchen.

The thunder drew closer, directly overhead. I felt how the rumble and the crack shuddered through me. I don't know how long I stood behind the bushes, but when I stopped shaking and opened my eyes, the kids on the street had all gone home. Lucky them. No one was pulling a knife on anyone at their house. A few minutes later when the rain started, I saw Bud bound up the front steps letting the screen door bang behind him.

The wind stirred the spiked branches of the spirea across my arms and bare legs. It felt good to be getting wet and scratched. Why didn't anyone call me in? I wanted to go in now but took a few more breaths to make sure I was okay before I slipped away from my safe spot and ran up the front steps.

They all looked up when I stepped into the living room. Bud was sitting cross-legged on the floor, cradling a bowl of ice cream and laughing with my father at a joke being told on the radio. My mother was in her chair with a basket of mending on her lap. Her eyes were red-rimmed from crying.

"There's a dish of ice cream for you in the freezer," she said. "It shouldn't be too icy to enjoy."

My father tipped the page of the newspaper down and smiled at me as though nothing had happened.

I wanted to punish them, go straight to my room, make Mom have to come in and ask me what was wrong. But, I didn't.

Instead I walked into the kitchen—now I thought of it as the blood red kitchen—and quietly opened the drawer to make sure that the knife was in the right place. The edge of the blade looked razor sharp, but I was too scared to touch it.

"Do you need help out there?" Mom called from the living room.

"No." The metal drawer squeaked as I eased it closed. I took out the bowl of vanilla ice cream studded with chunks of strawberries and stood still holding the coldness in my hands long enough to erase the image of the knife at my father's throat before I joined them back in the living room. I sat next to Bud on the floor, cross-legged like he was. We stayed this way, no one talking, only the radio playing, until Mom said it was my bedtime.

I went into the bathroom and closed the door. I brushed my teeth. Then I took the shiny cuticle scissor down from an open shelf. Turning it over in my hands, I spread the blades, and pressed a sharp tip against the soft skin of my pointer finger making the same triangle as on Dad's neck. *Unless you can finish the job ... .*

I pulled in a deep breath, held it, and jabbed the sharp tip into my skin, letting out my breath as a bubble of red bloomed.

I felt the pain and put my lips on the wound to suck the small hole I'd made in my fingertip and to taste the strange, metallic flavor. Then I put the scissor back on the shelf, leaving the blood on it.

Barbara Clarke's memoir, *Getting to Home: Sojourn in a Perfect House*, was published in 2009. Her essay "Good Vibrations," appeared in the online magazine *Full Grown People* in 2015. "Thank You, Grace Paley," and "Tis the Season" have been published through her participation in Red Wheelbarrow Writers. Forthcoming—*The Opposite of Hate: A Family Memoir.*

Blessed in Singapore

By Lisa Dailey

My husband Ray and I approached the ticket counter at the Kadena Air Force Base terminal in Okinawa, thrilled to see a flight to Singapore with 47 seats available.

"How can I help you today?" asked a young woman neatly attired in her pressed blue uniform, hair knotted at the base of her neck.

"We'd like to be marked present for the flight to Singapore," Ray replied.

Everyone in the military can take advantage of the Space Available program, Space-A for short. Military planes fly from base to base all over the world every day moving troops, equipment, and supplies. When there is extra space, the seats are offered up to those traveling for relocation, deployment, emergency, or even vacation. There is little to no charge for these flights, which made a world trip far more cost effective for our family of four than it would have been otherwise. Employed by the Public Health Service as a dentist, Ray was a member of the United States Uniformed Service, which allowed us the use of the Space-A program.

"Is Singapore your final destination?" the agent asked as she reviewed our passports and travel orders.

"We're actually taking several months to travel around the world with our family. Our goal was to get as close to mainland Asia as possible on Space-A flights, but we never imagined we'd get all the way to Singapore," I said.

We were taking time to travel, yes, but this trip was more than an extended vacation for me. I was fleeing seven years of continual loss accompanied by habitual and increasing alcohol use to numb the grief. My brother, father, and mother had all passed away. I had cared for my mother as she succumbed to an aggressive form of cancer. The change in her personality from chemotherapy and radiation had taken its toll on our family, and especially on me. Ray and I had been at odds as we tried to hold up under one stressor after another. Back home, I'd teetered at the edge of depression and even now, though I saw glimpses of my well-adjusted former self, I was anxious and fretful much of the time.

"I need to warn you that the air quality in Singapore is in the unhealthy range right now due to the fires in Indonesia," the agent advised.

"Yes, we've seen a bit of news coverage on the fires, but Indonesia is pretty far away from Singapore, isn't it?" Ray asked, always the optimist.

"Indonesia is about 700 miles to the south, but the smoke is affecting air quality in Singapore. Are you sure you want to get on the flight, sir?" she asked.

"Definitely," Ray responded. Making it all the way to mainland Asia translated into huge cost savings.

"This is a list of rules in Singapore," the agent turned back toward us and handed Ray a piece of paper. "I need to advise you to review this list with everyone in your party."

"Will do," said Ray handing the list of rules to me.

We settled into hard, plastic chairs in the waiting area and I pulled out the list of rules.

"Okay, boys, listen up. We need to review some rules," I said. "First, no selling gum. That one carries a $100,000 fine or two years in prison."

"What!?! A hundred thousand dollars?" asked Tyler. $100,000 was an absurd amount of money to a 15-year-old.

"Why would we sell gum?" RJ asked, always my inquisitive child.

"But we can chew gum, can't we?" Tyler added.

"I'm not sure why you would sell it," I replied. "It sounds like they don't like gum chewers so I would avoid gum altogether while we're there. Next, $1,000 fine for annoying someone with a musical instrument. Finally, a rule that will limit your singing, Ray!"

"Are you saying my voice is a musical instrument? That's so kind. I knew you liked my singing!" Ray beamed.

RJ, Tyler, and I groaned. The only admirers of Ray's singing were neighborhood dogs who all perked up and added to the chorus when Ray belted out a song.

"There's a $5,000 fine for flying a kite or playing any game that interferes with public traffic," I continued. "Three months in prison, a fine, or both for singing songs that have obscene lyrics."

"That does limit my options," Ray added.

"All right, c'mon everyone, let's finish the list," I said. "A $1,000 fine for spitting in any public place. Connecting to another user's wifi is deemed as hacking and carries a $10,000 fine, three years in prison, or both."

I could see both boys trying to work out what exactly this meant for their online pursuits and how they might get around the restriction.

"Listen to this one, boys. All boys," I said making sure I had everyone's attention. "Forgetting to flush the toilet is $150 fine."

"Who goes around checking that?" Ray asked.

"We're almost done. No feeding the pigeons. That is a $500 fine. And no urinating in a public elevator. This says that some public elevators have urine detection devices that set off an alarm and close the doors when any odor of urine is detected until the police arrive."

"What is urinating?" RJ asked.

"Peeing, RJ. No peeing in an elevator," I answered.

RJ and Tyler looked at each other and erupted in giggles.

"Alright, alright, one more," I continued. "No taking drugs before you enter the country. That one carries a $20,000 fine, 10 years in prison, or, in certain cases, the death penalty."

"Again, who is checking?" Ray asked with a roll of his eyes. "Do we have to give blood and urine samples when we enter the country?"

"Just make sure you're not in an elevator when you give your sample," I answered setting the list aside.

We boarded the flight and took off for Singapore, a small island nation at the base of Malaysia, just 88 miles north of the equator and essentially the southernmost point of continental Asia. We were shocked to see only seven passengers on the flight, including our family of four. Maybe the air quality was more concerning than we had imagined.

Landing in Singapore, the plane was engulfed by the thickest, brownish-orange smoke I had ever seen. Although mid-afternoon, the haze choked the sun's rays and made it feel like the sun had already set. We exited the plane and slammed into a wall of smoke and humidity that left us all feeling physically depleted and struggling to get enough oxygen. I worried we'd made the wrong decision to come here.

The Paya Lebar Air Base in Singapore was tiny. The terminal consisted of a single, walk-in-closet-sized room, with three chairs lining one wall and a small teller window at one end housing passport control. As we waited for our luggage to come in from the plane, I looked around for a Traveler Information Sheet listing recommended places to stay and dine in the area. I had grown accustomed to finding the sheets in all the U.S. military terminals we had visited. I only then realized that this was not a U.S. installation, but a Singaporean base used only as a refueling and staging site.

"Ray, I don't see any information on lodging," I said, my voice tight.

Since we hadn't expected to get to Singapore, we had failed to make any sort of hotel reservations. The lack of preparation along with the oppressiveness of the humidity and thick brown smoke ramped up my anxiety. The familiar comforts of U.S. terminals were non-existent—no place to lounge while waiting for flights, no air conditioning, and no helpful information sheet. For the first time, four weeks into our year of travel, we were truly on our own with no support from base personnel or anyone else.

"I don't either. Don't get worked up," Ray replied, as tired of my anxiety as I was. "Just sit for a minute and I'll go see what I can find."

He returned a few minutes later and told us he was able to find a hotel as well as a taxi company.

"We just have to walk off the base to meet the taxi," he said.

We trudged along in the oppressive heat, through barricaded gates flanked by Singaporean soldiers armed with automatic rifles into this apocalyptic-feeling, sweltering foreign land. Beads of sweat streamed down my back as we stood on the sidewalk waiting. Within minutes a taxi pulled over to pick us up and we were whisked away into Singapore.

"You want Princess Hotel?" the driver asked with raised, questioning eyebrows.

"Yes. That's the one," Ray replied.

"You take boys there?" the driver asked again, nodding in the direction of RJ and Tyler.

"Yes, all of us," said Ray.

I should have been a little suspicious that something was out of whack based on the driver's question, but the heat had sapped my energy. Nothing about the scenery indicated that we might be entering a less-than-savory part of town. In this tropical climate, paint seemed to bubble and peel off every building, old or new, giving them all a shabby, run down look.

As we unloaded our backpacks and headed toward the hotel entrance, I saw the taxi driver pull Ray aside and whisper something in his ear. We entered the lobby and began the check-in process, handing over passports and filling out registration cards.

"What did he say?" I asked Ray, who had become uncharacteristically quiet.

He avoided my eyes, "He said this was the red-light district of the city."

"Seriously? Is it safe here?" I asked with growing concern just as I had started to feel at ease.

"Very safe area," the hotel clerk chimed in. "All of Singapore safe, very little crime."

"It'll be educational," said Ray in his typical bubbly, always-the-optimist fashion. "We can teach the boys what's meant by 'red-light districts.'"

I rolled my eyes, but I didn't put up an argument. I decided to let myself be lulled into a sense of well-being by Ray and the clerk, though that was challenged after I found that the mattresses were covered with plastic sheets.

We stowed our belongings and set out to find dinner. The hotel clerk assured me again that it was perfectly safe to be out and about in the neighborhood and he gave us a few suggestions. Walking past a lady of the night, listening to Ray give a PG-rated, red-light district talk to the boys, I was reminded of that over-the-top, happy personality that I fell in love with.

Ray came bounding into my life one day as I was playing volleyball in the park. With his limitless enthusiasm and positive attitude, he was quickly accepted into the group and we became fast friends. Although my friends and family said I should consider dating Ray, I wasn't ready to head down that path. I had always pictured myself with someone more like Brad Pitt in *Legends of the Fall* – an athletic, sexy, resourceful mountain man. This skinny dentist with his half-mullet, crooked teeth, military-issued glasses and affinity for Star Wars wasn't the man I'd pictured spending the rest of my life with.

On a clear night one August, Ray and I walked to a nearby park, spread a blanket on the ground, and scanned the sky in search of the Perseid meteor showers. I'd forgotten my sweatshirt and had asked to borrow one of his. With little meteor action in the sky, Ray soon dozed off while I listened to his light snore mixed with the waves lapping on the rocks until the breeze off the water turned cold. When I started to shiver, I nudged Ray to wake him. He turned over on his side and gently laid one hand on my cheek.

"Are you cold? What time is it?" he mumbled, still groggy.

Although shocked by his touch, I chalked it up to him waking from a dream and didn't consider the gesture any further. We gathered our things and Ray escorted me to my car. I returned his sweatshirt, said goodnight, and drove away. As I pulled out of the parking lot, I glanced in the rearview mirror one last time and saw Ray close his eyes and slowly bring the sweatshirt to his face as if to breathe me in. My heart skipped a beat and I knew in that instant that Ray was "the one." He was a match for me intellectually, he challenged me in all the right ways, made me laugh and take myself far less seriously, and was my equal in sarcasm. He would always be my best friend and love me passionately, even if he didn't look like Brad Pitt.

Smack dab in the middle of the red-light district in Singapore, plastic sheets and ladies of the night, I smiled. I hadn't thought of that moment in a long time.

"See, this isn't so bad," Ray commented.

"Uh huh," I replied, letting go of my tightness just a little. "But you never get to make hotel reservations again."

I scolded myself for having been so anxious and unable to function under pressure. But I planned from that moment on to have at least one night booked in the city we were heading to so that we would not be left stranded or find ourselves in another red-light district.

The next morning, our first stop was the Singapore Botanic Gardens. On our way to the gardens, rain poured from the sky. Being from the Pacific Northwest, we were no strangers to rain, but tropical rain is completely different than the intermittent drizzle we knew. Rivers of water flooded down from the sky. By the time our taxi dropped us at the garden entrance, lightning and thunder rolled in enhancing the torrential downpour. We were not allowed in the gardens due to the proximity of the lightning. We sat under a large, open-air shelter with thatched roof and watched as lightning flashed all around us followed by booming thunder.

"Mom, look at my arms," Tyler said. The hair on his arms stood on end and I could feel mine doing the same.

"Holy shit!" Ray exclaimed as another flash of lightning struck just outside the shelter followed by a crack of ear-splitting thunder that vibrated through our bodies less than a second later.

"Dad, no swearing," RJ said with a worried look.

"The planes made rain," said a neatly-dressed, small Asian man sitting near us.

"Planes?" I asked, not sure I understood.

"Smoke so bad, planes put chemicals in clouds to force rain," he replied. "Rain help clear smoke."

The man explained that airplanes flew above the smog and dispersed chemical substances into the air with the intent to increase precipitation. As fascinating as this sounded, I started to worry about all those chemicals pouring down with the rain.

Before we could ask any more questions, the storm let up and we set out to tour the gardens. Since flowers don't hold much appeal for teenage boys or grown men for that matter, they all tired of the flowers after about 15 minutes. Much to their relief, the storms moved in again and our visit was cut short.

Our next stop was the Buddha Tooth Relic Temple and Museum, which claims to house the left canine tooth of Buddha, recovered from his funeral pyre in Kushinagar, India. There is no way that you can pass up a temple dedicated to a tooth when traveling with a dentist.

Thousands of artifacts and a plethora of information about Buddha are contained within a five-story, pagoda-looking red building. Making our way through the lower floors, we each found our personal guardian deity based on our zodiac sign and year of birth. We read that a personal guardian deity serves as a source of solace, spiritual support and inspiration. Simply having a personal guardian deity is not enough, however. One must actively work on purifying negative tendencies in order to strengthen our connection to our deity and speed our progress on a spiritual path.

How the hell do I go about purifying negative tendencies? I wondered. I would have paid money to purge the anxiety I'd been living with for the past several years.

We continued up to the highest floor in the temple to view the tooth. Meditation spaces flanked the sides of the room while meditation nooks made up the center space of the room. We walked down an aisle to a glassed-off area where the tooth of Buddha was housed in a 7,700-pound giant stupa made from 700 pounds of gold.

"Where is it?" RJ whispered.

"Is that it right in the middle?" I asked peering closer.

"I think so," answered Ray. "But it looks more like a molar."

A museum guide approached and led us to a monk dressed in the traditional Buddhist triple-saffron robe.

Crap. Were we being too loud?

The monk greeted us with palms pressed together and a gentle bow. The guide indicated that he wanted to sing a blessing for us.

Phew.

The monk did not speak to us but looked at each of us directly for a long moment. As I met his gaze, I felt as if he could see inside my soul and could feel the intimacies of my struggle and the heartache that I'd experienced. I felt a weight lifted off my chest and I could breathe a little easier. We were asked to kneel on the bare wood floor. The monk looked at each of us in turn as we said our names and then he proceeded to sing a blessing in a language that was foreign, yet soft and melodic.

As he began to sing, the pain in my knees faded as his words streamed into my thoughts. I thought about how I was living my life, stifled behind a smoke of grief and depression. I imagined how nice would it be if I could just sprinkle some chemicals into the dense cloud in my brain and wash away all my negative thoughts. Maybe this trip was my equivalent of cloud seeding. Maybe I needed more practice purifying my negative tendencies.

As the blessing continued, my legs started to tremble and I felt lightheaded.

Please don't faint, please don't faint.

And just as my thoughts shifted to keeping myself upright, the blessing ended.

I went to bed that night wrapped in my sleep blanket on top of plastic sheets in the red-light district of this smoky nation feeling at ease in the world. Had the monk's blessing helped to clear some of my clouded thoughts?

"How are you feeling about the trip so far?" I asked Ray as we searched for breakfast the next morning along a row of hawker stations.

"I think things are going really great," he replied. "How about you?"

"I think I feel happy," I said, after a few minutes of contemplation. I hadn't felt truly happy in years and I had to think hard about my state of mind before answering. "It seems strange to think that we've been traveling for more than a month now. And we really haven't been fighting." The realization suddenly hit me that we had not once bickered like we had so casually done at home.

"Honestly, I wasn't sure we'd even make it this far," he said, a light smile playing on his face. "I thought we'd be fighting a lot more too. What's changed for you?"

"I think I was incredibly miserable at home," I replied as we stopped for a moment to look at a menu. "I had a lot of loss and never had time to cope with one death before there was another. And the last two years of caring for my mom and watching her die really took a toll on my resilience. She was so mean after radiation. She broke my spirit, made me feel like nothing. I think our relationship suffered the consequences."

Ray watched me intently.

"But this is not one-sided," I continued. "You have changed too. What's different?"

"I think that we've left all the distractions of the world behind at home," he said after some consideration. "There is nothing to worry about here - no work, no school, no ferrying the kids from one event to the next, no schedules to keep, no bills to pay. All of the minor things that we bicker about are gone."

We continued walking, keeping Ty and RJ in sight.

"What do you think things will look like when we get back home?" Ray asked hesitantly.

"I don't know yet. For now, I am content being happy and exploring the world. Let's just start there and see what comes next." I wasn't ready to think about being back at home.

I couldn't help but feel that we were meant to come to Singapore, meant to learn about clearing the smoke with cloud seeding, meant to learn about purifying negative tendencies, meant to receive a blessing from a Buddhist monk. I needed to learn to let the clouds of grief empty themselves out.

Lisa Dailey is an avid writer and traveler. Her piece is from her upcoming memoir, *Square Up*, which details the adventures and misadventures of a seven-month trip around the world with her husband and two teenage sons as well as her own personal journey from grief into peace.

Mama

By Renée DeMont

Mama reached into the city trash can, pulled out a newspaper, and placed it under her arm. It wasn't wet; it would do. The air was chilly, crisp, not a cloud in the late night sky. The public bench, located just outside the YMCA, in downtown Los Angeles where Daddy would play cards tonight, was so cold our mother flinched as she set her fingers along the backrest of the gray porous slab and singed her free hand. Silencing a wince, Mama quickly blew wispy chutes of warm air across the tips of her fingers, in an effort to ease the sting. Startled, my three younger siblings and I stood just off to the side, along the curb of a vacant city street, concerned yet numb, as we watched Mama prepare our bed for the night. Weary, all five of us needed to lie down.

In another setting, Mama would have been considered beautiful. Scottish ancestry granted her the pretty contrast of alabaster skin and dark brown hair with auburn highlights, while faint traces of Cherokee Indian gifted her the noble high cheekbones of popular fashion models I had seen on the covers of magazines. I could see my mother was beautiful. Here though, Mama was simply another homeless woman on the streets of Los Angeles, blurry and insignificant.

Extending her arm, Mama let the worn strap of her saggy, black bag slide down her shoulder. She handed it to my seven-year-old brother Sean, without glancing back. The hefty bag was cumbersome; laden with the odd scattered contents I had managed to gather from the back seat of an old, yet reliable borrowed car we had been living in for the past two weeks. When Daddy complained earlier that his friend had grown impatient and demanded the car be returned that day, I scooped up everything I could. As the eldest child at eight, I had learned to scramble in times like these. Low and heavy as the bag was, my brother struggled to hike the flimsy strap up over his head. Finally he managed, placing his small hands on the bulk of the bag that hung down across his belly, keeping it close.

Everything we owned was in that bag: a short stack of clean cloth diapers, plastic pants, four diaper pins capped in yellow and pink cracked plastic, a dried up bottle of Cover Girl foundation Mama kept for days when she thought we might "see people," a deck of well-worn playing cards, a new unopened pack of Kool's cigarettes, a pair of footy pajamas, cuticle scissors, a man's black plastic comb, and recent racing form covered in notes and scribbles in blue. Also, from the last motel we stayed at: a handful of sugar packets, a silver book of matches with "Cloud 9" stamped on the front cover, and a ballpoint pen.

Eager to get inside the YMCA, Daddy stood facing us on the icy street, pensive, and impatient. Tobacco smoke filled my nostrils. Daddy wore his lightweight coat open. He shivered, but he smelled of sweat. With a hint of distracted purpose, he nodded at the two-year-old sleeping in my arms, "Nee, be sure and tuck that blanket up around your baby sister's head. Keep her warm." Obediently, I shifted the sleeping toddler from one arm to the next, struggling to stretch the baby-blue crocheted blanket from the top of her soft blonde curls, down around her legs.

Daddy's blue eyes were bloodshot as they grazed over my two younger brothers and me. His smile was weak, yet sincere. Loose slick strands of chocolate brown hair fell forward over his brow as he took a long drag off his cigarette, flipped the butt into the gutter, and blew a whistle of warmth into his cupped hands. Reaching up with splayed fingers, he combed the stray hair back across his scalp, centering himself.

My eyes marveled at the dark V of hair that came to a perfect point on the top of Daddy's forehead. At thirty-six, Daddy already had a prominent widow's peak. Ten years older than Mama, my parents looked remarkably similar in age. Life on the streets has a way of equalizing folks, making most adults appear the same age. The only trait that gave away Daddy's seniority was his premature receding hair line. I thought Daddy was handsome. I'm sure Mama thought so too. Never said as much, but I could feel the heat between them.

As if on cue, Mama reached under her sweater and withdrew a folded twenty-dollar bill from her bra, and placed it in the palm of Daddy's open hand. Anxious to get inside the building, he curled his fingers around the cash.

"Alright, let's do this," he said. Leaning over, he kissed Mama on the cheek, patted her behind possessively, and hustled into the YMCA.

My brothers and I watched Daddy turn and disappear into the lobby. The heavy door closed behind him with a thud, shutting in the heat. Mama took the dry newspaper from underneath her arm and slapped it swiftly across her thigh a couple of times, hard. Shards of broken silence shot out, filling the void between the skyscrapers that surrounded us. Mama's efforts effectively shook loose any stray bugs or random surprises that may have crawled between the sheets of paper.

Next, she took one section of the newspaper and opened it, spreading it across the seat of the stone bench. Then, another section, and then another, until the entire concrete surface was covered in overlapping layers of newspaper, tempering the harsh, blunt chill of the exposed stone. Satisfied with the makeshift bed, our young mother turned around, sat down in the middle of the bench, and opened her arms

"Okay babies, come here," she commanded with a soft weariness.

There was an elegance to our mother's reserved sadness; a sort of regal, efficient effort to be tidy amongst the turmoil. Sometimes, her sad eyes would rise half-mast and land on one of her four children. A light would seem to glow from behind her eyes; she would really see us.

Other times, a spark of unexpected inspiration would prompt a genuine smile. On the rare occasion, a rush of optimism would infuse her entire face with surprising hope. Those were the best of times, the times when Mama would gather the black comb and the tiny scissor she kept behind the zipper pocket of her black bag and go in search of a side mirror of a car, any car, to style her rich dark hair. The soil of the day often sullied the shine, but it was the order she longed for.

Mama kept her hair cut close to her head, parted down the middle, tucked behind her ears, and tapered to a neat point at the base of her neck. In spite of her sullen expression, most days there was a maturity to Mama's appearance that often mocked the youth of her twenty-six years. Tonight though, all rays of hope, dimmed by our dire circumstance, were lost on her deceptive beauty. Tiny buckets of shadows lay beneath her sunken hazel eyes; weariness, malnourishment, and the disappointment of the day were finally taking their toll. Frigid low temperatures outside made for a dangerous and miserable night's sleep, yet Mama set about making her homeless brood of four, all under the age of nine, as comfortable as possible.

While Mama saw to it we each had a coat of our own, the bulky, dark green, wool sweater she had on was all the wife of a friend could loan her. Oversized, it ran long past her waist and past her wrists too. Mama had always been thin, but she had gotten thinner since we lost the key to the motel room our family had been living in. We spent nine months in a row at the last motel, the longest stretch ever in one place all together. "Cloud 9" was on the sign out front. Daddy would laugh at the stupidity of other people who owned homes whenever we pulled into the parking lot.

"They're spending a fortune on a big house," he'd say, his voice exuberant, "when we live the life on Cloud 9!"

Life had almost been ideal, for a while. Daddy had a job then, not just Mama. We children attended school regularly, and we were presented with a home-cooked dinner most nights, or, at the very least, Mama would pull cash from her bag and send me down the street to bring back white paper sacks of greasy take-out goodness. We had friends and toys to play with too.

But the truth is, we didn't actually lose the key to the motel room. My family came home one day, and when Daddy parked the car in front of the motel room door, we could see a plastic thingy had been placed over the doorknob that prevented our key from working. This sparked a rage in Daddy. When Mama stepped back from the door in defeat, Daddy marched up to the office ready for a fight. Confident I could fix the problem, I walked up to the door and tried to pull the thingy off the handle. I tried and tried, but it just spun in circles. We were locked out. Daddy didn't like being reminded he was several weeks behind in the room rent. All the way up in the front office, everyone in the motel could hear Daddy's heated shouts as he cussed out the manager. Undeterred by our father's empty threats, the manager remained calm, firm. He followed Daddy back to our room and simply shrugged, "You can have your things back when you get caught up with the rent." All our possessions remained behind the locked door.

"I'll break the damn window!" Daddy shouted right in the manager's face, "You can't keep our things!"

Threatening to call the authorities, the manager glanced at Mama, offering a silent apology. She had been a reliable maid in his motel; I could tell he liked her, but, Daddy had taken her paychecks and gambled them away. There was nothing left to cover the lodging. Cutting off the manager's gaze of concern, Mama lowered her eyes and guided all four of us to the car. The smell of exhaust filled my nostrils. Daddy was already revving the engine. We piled into the back seat of the car as quickly as we could, then Daddy screeched out into the street.

"We'll be back, you son-of-a-bitch!" he'd yelled over his shoulder.

I stood up on my knees and looked out the dirty rear window as the motel faded from sight, certain Daddy was wrong. I knew we would never go back.

That was two weeks ago. Mama has worn the bulky, green sweater ever since. Hung loose around her thin thighs, it covered the top half of her brown denim jeans. Bare ankles rose above her feet, which were covered in a pair of faded navy blue tennis shoes. Provisional at best, puckered and worn, the thin dingy rubber peeled back from buff colored soles, in a state of retreat from too much wear and tear. Visibly drained, Mama never complained. I am sure her feet must have felt like boots of ice, but she remained patient as she tucked them under the newspaper-covered bench and waited, with open arms, for her offspring to join her.

Sean was always the first to step forward. He took his place to the left of Mama, using the soft black bag as a pillow. Flat on his back, he crisscrossed his legs, and tucked his hands under his armpits to keep them from freezing. My turn was next, but my kneecaps had turned to icecaps. I felt brittle and fragile, afraid if I moved my knees would shatter against the heavy stiff fabric of my new jeans. Donated, the pants were two sizes too big. Frigid air circulated beneath the loose denim and surrounded my boney legs, leaving me stiff and sore. Moving even a step or two filled me with irrational fear. I ached so bad from the cold, I thought my legs would shatter if I didn't stay perfectly still. Timmy, small for his four years, stood to my right, rubbing at his thick black lashes, about to drop and waiting for my lead.

My baby brother's desperate need to sleep helped me summon the courage to move. Carefully, I stepped forward. Bolts of pain shot through my frozen kneecaps and shattered my calm. Holding back tears, I handed the baby, and the warmth that came with her, over to our mother. Bone-chilling air rushed at my chest and exhaustion enveloped me. Newspaper crinkled beneath my body as I lay myself down on the other side of Mama. I reached out and grabbed Timmy's dark green jacket and tugged, pulling him close. Nudged his little body into the curve of my own, and tucked my throbbing knees into the backs of his legs.

"Use my thighs for a pillow," Mama instructed.

The denim beneath my cheek helped assuage my momentary discomfort. Mama was safe. Comfortable. Timmy's black hair looked blue in the moonlight and tickled my nose as I drew him closer. My baby sister, Kasha, was out cold against Mama's chest. Her little legs peeked out from under the crocheted blanket and braced on the bench, keeping her in place. I knew Mama and Kasha would prevent each other from freezing. Once Mama looked down and saw we were all settled in, she reached for the last of the newspaper she had hung over the back of the bench and spread it out, covering our bodies on either side of her. Then, we felt her arms reach out and rest heavily upon us, keeping the sheets of paper in place.

Newspaper for sheets wasn't what other people used to keep warm at night, like the families who were nice enough to take us in on occasion, but Mama assured her young lot, "It would do."

Most nights, I could fall asleep pretty quickly, exhausted from the drag of the day. Tonight, the frosty, unforgiving conditions made sleeping outside difficult. I squirmed, and the crystal stars overhead caught my attention. Arching backwards, I counted to twelve in my head. Twelve scattered stars shone down on my homeless family, a string of dot-to-dot light in the darkness of our sky. Entranced, I stared. Heard Gram's comforting reminder in my head, "Remember, the stars are there to wish upon."

Mama's mother, my Gram, taught me the stars were there when we needed help. Gram knew a little something about the challenges in life: at seventeen, she became a mother, at thirty-five, a grandmother. Motherhood had brought her little joy, she'd said, but her many grandchildren inspired her to be more intentional and considerate. Once I was old enough to attend school, Daddy bought me a pretty light blue outfit and shiny black patent leather boots, and left me with Gram for two years. I learned to read, to write, and also to tell time on the small grandfather clock that hung next to the front door in Gram's tiny, one bedroom house she rented in San Luis Obispo. Nearly a year had gone by since the last time I heard the heavy, brass hands of the wall clock strike the hour, and chime.

We were buddies, Gram and I. When Mama wrote to Gram on Cloud 9 motel stationary saying she wanted me back ("You've taken care of Renée long enough. I hope she hasn't been a bother?"), Gram decided I belonged to her daughter and that was that. I had to go. But before I left, Gram wanted us to have a special week, just her and me. The night she was free from the graveyard shift at the hospital, we took blankets and popcorn and went to the drive-in movie to see, *Willy Wonka and the Chocolate Factory*. During intermission, I held her hand and skipped to the bathroom. Returning to her car, Gram offered popcorn and we chatted lightheartedly about the trip I was to take to see Mama and Daddy. Suddenly, concern flooded her words, "Do you want to go? Your mother lives six hours away..." I didn't know how far that was, but Mama had written me a letter too, and it was filled with exciting news about my new baby sister that "...was one already!" She wrote about what a good big sister she thought I would be, and how she needed my help, "...she looks like you, Nee." Then Mama explained, "The boys are in a foster home, but we are trying to get them back." I loved my family, but I did not miss them. I preferred to stay with Gram. Excited to see a new sister though, I nodded with sincere anticipation when Gram asked again, "You sure now?"

Just before the next movie began, Gram set the popcorn aside, placed the window speaker back in its cradle and pulled me onto her lap. Pointing at the sparkly stars up in the sky, she began to teach me the nursery rhyme:

> *Star light, star bright,*
> *The first star I see tonight,*
> *I wish I may, I wish I might,*
> *Have the wish I wish tonight.*

We recited the poem together, until I got it down. "See those stars way up there? They are just like that night-light I leave on in the bathroom at home. Those stars brighten up the sky to make us feel safe...and, you know what? They're always there! No matter how far you go, you and I will share the stars." Gram winked, and we both giggled. I turned and wrapped my arms around her neck. We stared up at the stars and Gram whispered in my ear, "What's your wish?" I made a wish that night to see my new baby sister. I already had everything else. Soon, my wish would come true.

A year later, lying on a stone cold bench beside my sister, using newspaper for sheets, I found comfort in the sparkly stars above and wound my arms tighter around my little brother. I yawned and thought about those stars. Daddy needed their help. I needed to make a wish.

"Daddy's going inside," Mama had informed us earlier, "...up on the top floor...to try and win some money." Playing poker, I surmised.

Daddy was really good at poker. He played for a living. He won big, and he won often. He was a high roller and had won millions over his lifetime. Told us often that only the most skilled players were granted access to card games with high stakes; only the most formidable, shrewd players with the highest, most respected reputations were allowed entry. Competition was the rush. If you won, you left feeling high, because you had earned it.

Daddy told us he gambled with famous people sometimes, and three weeks ago I asked who he was going to play against next. He picked me up and swung me around. His blue eyes crinkled with happiness and I wondered if my blue eyes looked the same as he answered, "Telly Savalas! Hoo-wee, is he good at poker!" he exclaimed. "Remember? He plays that detective on television, the one with the bald head...but his real name is Telly."

I wrapped my arms around his neck as he held me in our room at the Cloud 9.

"Can I go with you? I wanna see the bald man from TV!"

The television had been on every night until it went static; I knew which detective Daddy was talking about. Deep laughter filled the air. Daddy felt invincible when he was around famous people.

"Baby girl, of course you can go," he proclaimed after kissing my cheek. "YOU are Daddy's good luck charm!"

I adored my father, but I discovered later that night, I didn't like that man from the television.

"You brought your kid?" he barked, looking scarier than he did on TV. I wanted to go home. Even though I buried my face in Daddy's dark brown polyester pant leg, he was determined to join in the game. Boldly Daddy shrugged off the angry bellow from the bald man and peeled me from his pant leg. Plopping me down in a gold, velvet overstuffed chair, he tousled the top of my head and motioned, "Shhh..."

I sat there a long time. Wide-eyed and fearful, I felt my lids grow heavy with nervous exhaustion, longing to draw themselves shut. Willing Daddy to win wore on my emotions. My eyeballs grew itchy with the sting of cigar smoke, pleading with me to let them rest. Lopsided, my head hung from side to side. Avoiding eye contact with the men at the poker table, I turned quietly and slowly onto my side, curling my stiff legs underneath my body. I buried my face in the plush fabric of the back of the chair, and passed out. Daddy lost to the bald-headed man and his friends, lost all our rent money, and now we were on a freezing bench waiting.

A similar kind of unbearable fatigue consumed me now as I searched out the brightest stars in the night sky. I may be only eight, but my experience had already taught me: sometimes, what we do today, often counts more tomorrow. I wondered if Daddy was playing cards upstairs with the same bald television detective again and shuddered. Even the heat from our huddled bodies couldn't prevent the chill that ran through me as I twisted backward on the bench. Looking up at the building, I hoped he wasn't.

Four giant red letters and two upside down triangles stood high, spelling out YMCA across the top of the tall brick building behind our bench, beckoning to all: enter, and find respite. But it wasn't open to all; the YMCA was for men only. No women or children allowed. Fatigue threaded my brows prompting them to lower. I blinked and let my focus fall just below the lighted sign. Only light flickered from the windows above. I closed my eyes, and wished hard under my breath saying the poem Gram taught me.

Star light, star bright,
The first star I see tonight,
I wish I may, I wish I might,
Have this wish I wish tonight: Please let my Daddy win.

I exhaled as I handed over the fate of our predicament to the bright comforting stars in the sky. Mama noticed I was still awake and tugged on my collar. I rolled away from thoughts of Daddy, towards Mama.

"Go to sleep," she whispered as she tucked the collar of my coat up around my face. Mama's fingers were so cold, red, and chapped. The bitter chill of winter seeps in with flagrant disregard for anyone's well-being. I shifted closer. Mama needed to be warm too.

The scent of printed ink and Mama's stale perspiration lined my nostrils as I drifted off to sleep. Finding solace in the familiar, my rigid, clenched bones melted into a soft lump of flesh. For the moment, the paralyzing weight of living on the streets and the agony of the bitter cold drifted away along with my worrisome thoughts.

I love you, Mama. I love you, Daddy. I love you, Gram. I love you, twinkly stars above.

Renée spent much of her childhood in extreme poverty, homeless and in foster care. As a resilient young woman, she became a successful entrepreneur and raised two thriving children. Now she is a published writer for Feminine Collective, and looks forward to the publication of her first memoir titled, *A Careless Man's Careful Daughter.*

Séan Dwyer

The "What-Ifs"

By Séan Dwyer

February, 2015

In my dream, two young men step into the crosswalk in front of my stopped car. They are wearing light jackets, one with a checked flannel shirt under his. One nods his thanks to me for stopping. They have walked down a steep stairway from a row of condos that overlooks Bellingham Bay, and they are headed to another set of stairs that will take them down the bluff to Boulevard Park, beside the Bay. They chat, engrossed in whatever plans they have for when they descend the stairs on the other side of the road.

They pass my passenger-side headlight and have reached the point of no return. My rearview mirror, which had been reflecting the low-hanging January sun, suddenly fills with a black rectangle. A second later, a shattering *bang!* fills my head, and my front tires roll over one man, while my bumper throws the other into the air. I then feel my rear tires run over the first man again, while my front tires crush the second man just as he lands.

I start awake, and my torso jerks upward as I try to sit up and catch my breath. The bruised, swollen stalk of my neck is so weak that I can't lift my head off the pillow. The pain I feel in that moment will dog me all day. I ease back onto my mountain of pillows and try to relax.

A month into this experience, I have been oversharing about my accident everywhere I go, and a common refrain people say is, "at least you didn't hit the pedestrians." I agree that I am fortunate not to have that guilt on my shoulders, and also that I don't have to feel bad for the driver who hit me. He would have pushed me into them if they had not seen him coming. His life would have been damaged more than mine has been.

I lie here in the dark at four AM, manipulating my head with both hands into a comfortable position, at an angle that will put less stress on the stretched ligaments and sprained muscles in my upper back and neck. I want to feel anger that, even though I "didn't hit the pedestrians," I still face the trauma nightly in my dreams, as if I had smashed into them. I don't feel anger, because I don't feel emotions yet. When I learn of bad news, I say, "That's really sad." But I don't feel the pain I expect. Now, I don't feel excited that my brain is waking up enough to give me my first dreams, because if this is what dreaming will be from now on, I'm not sure I want any part of it.

My pulse slows, and I reset the audiobook I am using to distract my brain from slipping into ruminations and obsessions. I fall asleep, and that particular nightmare doesn't return. I awake in the morning relieved to be rid of it.

July, 2015

I have known about the Brain Injury Alliance of Washington, Bellingham Chapter, for a couple of months. My wife, Maureen, also knew about it, thanks to her work in the public sector. She had suggested that I wait a few months before attending a meeting, so I did. But now it's time for me to start going.

We are meeting in the dank basement of a Peace Health building on Chestnut Street. Mary, a nurse nearing retirement, runs the meeting. We, the Traumatic Brain Injury (TBI) Survivors, fill both sides of three eight-foot tables. The westering sun blasts through the windows, and no one in this group has the physical capacity to close the decrepit blinds. There are several men here, but I am the steadiest on my feet, and I can't handle the strain of pulling on the cords. Between the sun and the fluorescent overhead lights, my dark glasses are nearly useless, and I bow my head.

Mary calls the meeting to order. She has us introduce ourselves. I learn quickly that I am not the only Survivor who notes the date and time of my accident. For all of us, the moment our brain became something different is the moment our old selves died. Many cannot talk well. Many cannot walk well. Many start a sentence and can't remember how to finish it. One or two can't stop talking.

One woman interrupts people's bios to compare her experiences to theirs. Mary makes a general stern reminder that we need to raise our hands before we speak. Conversations derail easily here.

Some say they can't sleep. Some can't stay awake. After the introductions, we have a contest to win Independence Day swag. Mary gives us basic multiplication problems we have to do in our heads. For many, this exercise is the toughest cognitive challenge they can handle and still succeed. I win a flag-themed hard-plastic drinking glass that comes with its own permanent hard-plastic straw. Some others would find more need for this glass, as I learn over time.

I see why Maureen wanted me to wait until I saw personal progress before I joined forces with these Survivors. Many of them have been in recovery for several years.

After the meeting, I'm sad. And scared of what the future holds. As I do several times a day, I review the accident in my mind. This time, for some reason, I get stuck on thinking about the "what-ifs." What if I had turned my head the wrong way during the crash, and I suffered injuries that prevented me from talking properly or moving freely? Or what if I could not have regained enough brain function to return to work when my six-month leave ended? As it was, I'd taught several mock classes to get myself into shape for teaching a summer course. What if I'd had to retire? What if I hadn't been able to write again?

As I carefully drive home (I will always be more than reasonably careful when driving now), I decide I'll throw myself into being supportive of my TBI peers because I feel gratitude that I am not facing the struggles some of them endure. I also feel guilt that for reasons that I cannot take credit for, I fared better than they did.

August 3, 2017

More than two years have passed since I won my flag-themed grown-up sippy cup. I'm sitting at my desk at home, the blinds down as usual, soft music in my earphones. I'm drinking coffee and crunching budget numbers in the sluggish way I've grown used to moving. When the numbers begin to do the backstroke, I switch windows from the spreadsheet to the folder I have named "Bye Bye Civic," the collection of photos of my accident. I am supposed to scrutinize the photo Maureen took from the passenger's side of my crushed Civic so my lawyer understands everything that went on during the collision. We are still trying to get a fair settlement.

I have examined this photo ad nauseam, because I still cannot believe that this little metal rectangle held up under the force of the impact. After all this studying, though, I still learn something new today. I see that my headrest bent backwards due to my head slamming into it. I stare at the headrest, at the twin steel prongs that my head wrenched partially from their mooring in my seat.

When my seat snapped flat and the back seat surged under it and slammed me toward the sky, my head whipped forward on my neck, my chin cracking into my sternum. Hitting that hard against the headrest, what was to keep me from breaking my neck? From shattering my skull? From bleeding to death internally? What if any one of those scenarios had played out?

I shiver. I have to look away. Rather than go back to my budget, which doesn't seem too important at the moment, I distract myself with Facebook. Clicking on cat videos and writing a couple of birthday wishes will clear my head.

A new post pops up from an author friend. She is doing a survey for a plot point.

The question is, "Do you know how to drive a stick?"

I write without thinking, "Yes, and it saved my life."

I reply to a message from another friend, and then I return to my budget work. I'm sorting the utility bills when I freeze.

It saved my life. Why did I just write that driving a stick saved my life? I look back at the photo of my totaled car. Somewhere inside me I know why I believe what I wrote, but I can't follow my thoughts beginning to end. As I strain to push through the logjam, my frontal lobe tingles. My brain slows and so does the flow of oxygen. My temples ache. My neck tenses up, and my eyes begin to burn despite the low light.

My jaw slackens, and I start to wheeze. I sustained three whiplashes in three seconds. No wonder my neck still hurt months later. Another sinister "what-if" begins to coalesce. I could be a quadriplegic now, unable to type these thoughts. I could be too damaged to think them at all. Much of my thinking over these two years has been haunted with the "what-ifs" I build in my own mind every time I look at this picture.

I gaze at the photo, still trying to remember why I think driving a stick that day saved my life. This steadfast little Civic never failed to start in seven Minnesota winters. It never had to be pushed out of snow. The engine was still purring quietly when I reached forward and turned it off for the last time. I had been sure we would get past our 227,000 miles together, up to 300,000.

But it wasn't to be. Suddenly all the "what-ifs" I've ever entertained swirl through my mind like the ghosts outside Scrooge's window. Like those phantasms, some of them carry heavy chains, mountains of baggage. The combined weight on my soul leaves me staring at the photo, no longer seeing the image, but seeing through it to another multiverse where the "what-ifs" are realities.

"What if I hadn't stopped?" Those pedestrians were waiting patiently. They didn't step out to block me. On such a dangerous road, they had no intention of darting into the crosswalk. In this scenario, I would still be the person I was. I don't know if I would be better off that way, because Seán 2.0 is more aware of the need to use every day to its fullest. I'm sorry-not-sorry (today) that I put my foot on the brake.

The summer after the accident, I happened to meet a personal-injury attorney, and she told me she had litigated a similar scenario: her client was stopped at a light on a four-lane highway. The car behind his saw the red light and began to slow from 55, the speed limit. The third car in line was driven by an intoxicated driver. He became impatient when the car in front of him slowed, so he buzzed around it. He had no idea the light was red, and he plowed into the stopped car at sixty miles per hour, no brakes.

I asked the attorney how her client was doing after being hit at sixty. I was hoping to be comforted by the knowledge that he was well and had no brain injury.

"He's dead," she said. I detected a lilt of surprise in her voice, as if I should have realized on my own that being rear-ended at sixty was a death sentence.

What if the SUV that hit me had been going just a little faster than it was?

Then, at last, my mind circles back to the question of how driving a stick saved my life. The answer hits me with as much force as the Land Cruiser did. What if I had been driving an automatic? My Civic rolled 136 feet. My head drops into the palms of my hands, their heels pressing against my cheekbones.

But I do not cry. I am unable to make tears, more than two years into this odyssey.

A wave of understanding washes over me, and I know why I wrote that the manual transmission saved my life. When I stopped the Civic, I put it in neutral and took my foot off the clutch. The young men stepped into the crosswalk, then backed away. All this time, the SUV was bearing down on me.

The bumper of the Land Cruiser plowed into me and through my trunk, hard enough to roll me 136 feet. If I had been driving an automatic, or if I'd had my car in first gear, the transmission would have locked the wheels in place, and the rubber would have resisted the asphalt. I would have skidded a few feet forward, with the Land Cruiser grinding farther into my rear end the whole time. The trunk and back seat would have encroached more on my driver's seat, and the upward catapult would have been far stronger.

The disengaged transmission was the key to my survival.

I look online and find a calculator that estimates the force that hit me: 29,000 pounds. I'm not sure what that means, but I don't need to understand the physics to know I was hit hard. That long, slow roll, most of which I spent lying unconscious, absorbed much of the force.

If my car had not rolled, the result would have been paralysis or death. There's no way to deny it.

And so, a decision I made in May, 2003 to buy a five-speed Civic saved my life on January 29, 2015, at 3:42 PM. I think about time paradoxes, and visitors from the future, and parallel universes described in quantum physics theories. I bought my Civic because a friend bought one, and I liked her car better than the Chevy Cavalier I had at the time. I chose my five-speed Civic over an automatic. Did a version of my friend come from the future to buy her car so I would buy one just like it to save myself from death? Did a merciful God put the thought in my head so I would survive this accident twelve years later?

I don't know, of course, but if so, did "I survive for a reason?" I don't mind repaying the cosmos for keeping me alive, even with this awful cognitive slowness that frustrates me daily, but I don't think I can live up to the pressure of figuring out the reason I survived.

I know that my situation could be worse. Every time I hear "well, at least . . ." about the pedestrians, or my fragile but not broken neck, or my relatively good cognitive progress, those thoughts have already crossed my mind. Maybe I don't mind hearing those words because I *want* my accident to be diminished; I want it to be a little bump on the bumper, a thump on the noggin, and a transitory pain in my neck. If that's the case, I'll be better in a few days and ready to rock my second life as Seán 2.0.

But dang, two years have passed, and I keep re-enacting scenarios of events that actually didn't even happen. I want to scream, *"When will this end?"* I want to break down in tears and let go of nightmares of things that might have happened but didn't. What if I could do that? What if I could let go of what happened and what didn't happen?

What if I could cry? I don't know. I can't even remember what it's like.

Seán Dwyer is the author of several published short stories. The memoir from which his piece is adapted, *A Quest for Tears: Surviving Traumatic Brain Injury,* published by Penchant Press International, is forthcoming in January 2019. He is an avid supporter of the writing community; he is president of Whatcom Writers and Publishers, and he runs a monthly Open Mic at Village Books in Bellingham, Washington. He lives in a green house with his lovely wife and their hairless cat. In his spare time, he teaches Spanish at Western Washington University.

Small Steps to Destiny

By Mary Jane Fraser

I was hungry. For love. For attention. For freedom from the bleakness of my teenage life. Then I met him and life suddenly seemed to have its own sun. He was handsome and smart but most of all, he loved me. Loved me.

Robin was my boyfriend for a year and a half. Then, I got pregnant, quit school and married. At 16 I stood beside my soon-to-be husband at our small wedding ceremony, just the two of us and a random witness in a place that provided quick marriage services. I believed I was going to have a good and safe life.

I was delighted to have our big blue-eyed baby, and in a year and a half, she was joined by a younger brother. But a second child made me feel like we had to get serious about creating our future. We had to stop playing at grown-up life and start thinking about money and structure and buying a home.

Robin was seven years older than I. He worked as a draftsman at the Boeing Company, but had trouble keeping his job. He loved jazz music, philosophy, and crossword puzzles, but my husband also loved alcohol.

One night when our two little ones were finally asleep, Robin and I sat on the sofa in our two-bedroom apartment. I curled up my feet under me. And then I said, "Listen, we have to get serious." We talked and talked until the words just stayed in my mouth, clogging my throat, choking me.

Since that conversation had gone so badly, I never talked to Robin about our future again. Instead, I worked as hard as I could to keep the children fed and to use the little money he brought in as wisely as I could. I kept thinking if I just did enough, pleased him enough, he would find it in himself to stop drinking. I was too young to know that I could not get more of my needs met by doing more for someone else.

One hungover morning, I tried to awaken Robin so he could get up and have the breakfast I'd made for him: bacon, hash browns, eggs and toast. It was on the table as was his lunch to take to work. But he didn't want to get up. I kept pacing between the kitchen and the bedroom, imploring him to get out of bed. He kept pulling the covers up and tucking them under his chin, laughing. For some reason, he thought this was funny.

Nothing was funny to me. I was 18 years old with two children. I had no skills, no income, no support, and no idea what to do with a drunk husband.

At 9:30 AM, long after Robin ought to have been at work, I stood by the side of the bed in complete exasperation. The spring sunlight was coming through the window. Little green leaves peppered with pink flowers brushed across the window above our bed. The springtime beauty was such a contrast to my despair. Still, I refused to resort to tears; I was frozen to my spot, completely still, struck by a slap of reality. I heard my inner voice say

"This is it. This is your life. This is your future."

As if I had left my body, I could see the timeline of my life stretching into the future. Women didn't leave their husbands much in those days. Once you were married, you were stuck.

"Yep, this is what you signed on for."

The next thought surprised me. It must have come from someplace deeper than my history or my understanding of the duties a woman had in a marriage. I heard some part of me rise up:

"Oh no this will not be my life! This will not be my future. No. It goddamn will not."

I want to say I was angry, but that's not really what I felt. In my childhood household, there was no support for the kind of healthy confidence I was feeling as I stood in the bedroom looking at my drunk husband. But I'd managed to garner praise elsewhere over the years, mostly in school. And adults who'd seen what was good and strong inside of me had infused me with the idea that my life could mean something.

I drew in my breath and stood up taller. Robin remained asleep, oblivious that a decision was happening in his presence. I knew I would have to muster all of the confidence I could as I faced a future I had no model for.

I heard sounds from the children's room, so I went to tend to them. Carmen, my beautiful little girl, was still soundly sleeping but Brent was stretching as the new day began. I knew I had to protect them from Robin's carelessness. I was overwhelmed by sorrow and fear, but I picked up Brent, my four-month-old baby, and nuzzled his ear, telling him I would fight for them. I would make a life for them that was better than this. Somehow, we were all going to grow up.

I never expected to feel such hot, steeliness and clarity as I determined that I would have to find my good life some other way than I'd planned. This refusal of the future that I could see I would have with Robin was arguably my first volitional act of self-esteem. That one decision, the decision to take a hold of my life and make it what I wanted began in that one early morning sunlit moment.

Later that morning, Robin finally got up and came into the kitchen. I was waiting for him there and spoke before I lost my nerve. "Robin. Robin, look at me."

"I'm just getting breakfast."

"Ok, get your breakfast but I want you to hear what I have to say. I won't do this with you. You've tried to stop drinking and you can't do it and I can't continue being the wife of an alcoholic, not anymore. You've made it impossible for me to continue. I am going to move out."

"Can we talk about this later?" he said. No doubt his head was pounding and the late afternoon light would feel like a spotlight in his eyes.

"You know what?" I said, "No. No, we can't talk about this later. I'm done talking. I have nothing new to say. You've heard it all before anyway." I said this even though I still had some small hope that with time, Robin might gain strength, come to his senses, and keep his promise to be my husband. I suppose some part of me hoped that maybe separating would be enough

to jar him into committed action. The truth was I couldn't imagine being without him. But I also refused to imagine life going on day after day with him drunk, passed out, or otherwise
checking out of family life.

That same day, I got a newspaper and looked at available
rentals. While leaving was daunting, I thought I could do it. I
had to have some money just to get by, so I packed my babies
into the car and went to the welfare office and signed up for
services to help me stay afloat until I found a job.

Next I went to the employment office where I took a bunch
of tests to determine my achievement levels and capabilities,
including how quickly against the clock I could put washers on
rivets—just in case I went to work building Boeing airplanes.
My test scores were excellent. Who knew I was so smart?

I found a place to live with the children, but I'd never lived
alone. Ever. Day after day I had to face an aloneness that truly
scared me. Each morning I awoke and wondered how I was going to provide for myself and my two tiny children. At night, I
cried myself to sleep with panicked images of homelessness if I
couldn't find work and learn to take care of us all. But as the
weeks marched on, I was beginning to feel—not hope or wish or
even to dream, but to feel—something new. Strength. I started
to really imagine that I could make choices that would draw me
toward a life that suited me, one task by one task.

Facing the mountain of fear and self-doubt in front of me
left me trembling—often. I encountered the censure of both
families. I didn't know the AA caution about taking it one day at
a time, but the slogan was completely fitting for me. One day
was about all I could manage.

Then about three months after leaving my marriage I got
notice that the good souls at the Employment office had seen
something in me and had quietly become my advocates inside
of a system that usually pitied young single women with children. They'd gotten in touch with someone from the Division of
Vocational Rehabilitation and through some maneuvers I will
never know the truth of, the Employment office staff had arranged for Vocational Rehabilitation to pay my tuition to attend
college.

So, much to my total surprise, the girl who hadn't been allowed to finish high school was going to go to back to school. To college. Me. Full time. Me.

A new future was taking shape for me: one in which I could be in charge of my own destiny.

Mary Jane Fraser found nurturance and strength in overcoming obstacles by striving to overcome a childhood of neglect. She is proud to belong to the small group of people (statistically) who does not have a high school diploma but who has fulfilled the tasks for a Doctoral degree. Because of her love of learning, she has made the world her textbook and enjoys writing about her travels.

The Phases of My Womb

By Colleen Haggerty

Phase I. New Moon

When I was a pre-teen I was eager to get my period, not because I wanted the responsibility of my monthly bleeding - or the inconvenience, like I had overheard my two older sisters complain about. I wanted my period so I could feel older. Mature. Like a woman. I imagined I'd walk down the street with confidence, wearing nylons and high heels, tossing my hair behind my shoulder with a care-free, confident attitude.

The day came unexpectedly, like it does for all of us, the summer of my twelfth year. I was at Jenny's house, a girl I didn't know that well, waiting for my mom to pick me up. I went to the bathroom to pee and saw, for the first time, that tell-tale sign that my period had started: a bright red spot on my white underwear. Mom had talked to me ad nauseam about my impending period so I was mentally prepared, but I wasn't physically prepared. From the toilet I stretched over to the cupboard below the bathroom sink and surreptitiously opened it to see if there were any Modess pads, like my sisters used. Nothing but Comet, Lysol, a sponge, and extra rolls of toilet paper. Sweat beaded on my brow and I looked around, panicked. I was going to have to use toilet paper.

As I wadded up a bunch to stuff in my underwear with shaking hands, I watched a small drop of blood drip into the toilet water which was already tinged yellow by my urine. The blood spread across the water like a science experiment at school and I wondered how blood molecules were different from water and urine molecules to make it do that.

Sitting on Jenny's bed waiting for Mom, I was distracted, fearful that I would bleed all over her bed. Instead of sitting cross-legged like I usually did, like Jenny was, I sat with my legs together, feeling conspicuous and silly. I put my folded hands in my lap to give my crotch double protection. My face was hot and prickly with embarrassment. As Jenny talked, I was only half listening to her, the other half of me was willing my Mom to drive up at any minute.

Mom finally arrived and I got in the car as quickly as I could. As she was backing out of the driveway, I blurted it out, "I just started my period."

Mom slammed on the brakes, turned to me, grinning from ear to ear and shouted, "What?! Really?" Jenny's mom, who was walking back into the house after escorting us to the car, stopped and turned to see what was going on.

"Moooooom, please keep driving. Pleeeeeeaaaaaase," I couldn't help but whine. I was mortified.

Mom started driving again, but put her hand on my knee, "Oh, honey, that's so great," she sighed. "My baby girl is a woman today." Getting my period didn't make me feel like a woman, it made me feel like a dirty, incompetent child.

But she called me a woman.

The seats in our Ford station wagon were vinyl, so my fear of making a bloody, irreparable mess was slightly alleviated. I puffed up my chest a bit and tried to hide my smile. *I am a woman.*

When we got home, Mom pointed me in the direction of the maxi pads and told me to get a belt from my older sister. In the bathroom, my sister explained how to put on the belt and how to attach the pad to the belt. I spent about a half hour in there figuring it all out on my own. I put on the belt, attached the pad and zipped up my shorts, but walking around felt like I imagined wearing a full diaper would feel. So I pulled my shorts back down and repositioned the pad, but it still felt too wide and cumbersome. I was afraid one of my three brothers would be able to notice the big bulge in my shorts. I could only imagine their merciless teasing. When I decided I had put the pad on correctly, I emerged from the bathroom quietly and walked up and down the hallway. I was alone upstairs so I was safe from ridicule. I kept pacing back and forth, trying to mold the pad to the shape of my crotch.

"Colleen, come on down, honey, Dad's home," Mom shouted from downstairs. I went to the top of the stairs and shouted back, "Aw, Mom, do I have to?"

"Come on," she said, coaxing me down the stairs with her warmth and love. I skipped down the stairs to try and look carefree and confident, but I tripped on the last stair. Mom didn't seem to notice. Instead, she linked her arm through mine and walked me out the front door into the warm evening air. Dad was just getting out of his car when we arrived. Mom looked up at Dad, her eyes glinting with pride, and said, "Dave, our baby girl is a woman today." She presented me to him with flourish, sweeping her arm wide; he accepted me into his arms and hugged me. "That's wonderful, Toot. Congratulations."

I let my head rest on his chest and breathed him in, a mixture of pipe smoke and sweat. "Thanks, Dad," I mumbled, not sure what else to say. But inside my heart was pounding. With pride that my body was doing the right thing. With fear for the unknown future.

Phase II. Waxing

We called it the curse. I had developed a love/hate relationship with my period. I loved that, for the last two years of junior high school, my period was my monthly excuse to escape the girl bullying that made me break into a cold sweat as I walked down the hallways between each of my classes, trying to look invisible.

When I couldn't stand the torments anymore, I called Mom at work complaining of cramps, telling her I needed to go home. Mom always sounded irritated when I told her about my cramps - but no wonder. She didn't know what I was going through. I was too ashamed to tell her that my entire class whispered behind my back about how my friend Denise and I were lesbians. All I wanted was a few days to myself every month to go home, eat peanut butter and jelly sandwiches and watch *The Price Is Right*. My period was my monthly savior, my free ticket out of that place. I didn't care that I had to walk the two miles from school to home. Even walking home in the rain was better than dealing with the cruelty in the hallways: girls barking at me, their way of letting me know they thought I was a "dog."

But I hated that my flow was unpredictable and often caught me off guard. Some months my flow was like a neap tide and I could relax, but some months my flow was like the spring tide: full, ripe and strong.

Once on a warm, sunny spring day in college, my boyfriend and I were walking through campus. We stopped on a grassy knoll to people-watch and soak in the sun. When we stood up, I felt what I thought was the dampness from the grass. I reached behind, brushed my rear-end and saw the red tinge on my fingers. A red spot the size of Montana on the back of my crisp, white pants announced to the world that I was on my period. We were a good ten minute walk from my dorm room; my boyfriend walked closely behind me as I hung my head in shame the entire way.

In my twenties, I was working at a non-profit that supported adults with developmental disabilities to live independently. After a meeting that went on for far too long, I stood up and felt the gush. I had flooded. A red spot, this time the size of Texas. swamped the blue woven chair. Shaking from panic and shame, I rushed to the bathroom to clean myself up. Then I talked to my supervisor to tell her what happened. I assumed I would get support, perhaps we'd even laugh about it. Instead she said, with an admonishing tone, "Oh, Colleen, that's something one of our clients would do." She then gave me step-by-step instructions for removing blood from upholstery. I went back to the conference room, stacked a bunch of other chairs on top of mine and came back to work the next morning an hour early, upholstery cleaner and a pile of rags in hand, to clean up my mess.

Twice in my twenties, once when I was twenty years old and again when I was twenty-five, I found myself on the toilet, day after day, searching for the familiar red spot that would assure me that I hadn't completely fucked up, that I was safe from pregnancy. Both times I was so angry at my body for not protecting me, for allowing that to happen. Both times, I was confronted with the self-loathing and disgust in the decision I made. Both times I endured the high-speed sound of the vacuum as it sucked the life right out of me.

In my late twenties I started studying herbalism and alternative health care. Inherent in these studies was the assumption that all the functions of a female body—including the embarrassing leakage—were normal, even sacred. I charted my daily physical symptoms, from bloating and tender breasts, to cramps and irritability, and compared them month-to-month until I was able to predict their arrival. I stopped using tampons for a few years and relished the feel of my blood flowing out of me; I even grew fond of my blood's metallic smell. I tracked my cycle with that of the moon's and considered that perhaps there was a lunar pull to my womb. I nourished myself with herbs I harvested and dried myself: nettle, mug wort, St. John's wort. I discovered that my monthly cycle wasn't a curse, it was a blessing.

Phase III. Full Moon

Though I married when I was thirty-six years old, I was still unprepared and reticent when I became pregnant only six months later. I was terrified, not sure that I could be a good mother since I'd already snuffed out two lives. Could I really do it? Could my body really get me through a pregnancy?

After a day of thinking about it, I said yes. Yes to the unknown, yes to a prayer, yes to the dream I'd had since I was a little girl.

As it turned out, I could do it. I was amazed at how quickly and innately my body took over. My tender breasts prepared for the vital job of becoming a milk factory. Then my belly swelled like a tight balloon. After just a few months into my pregnancy I decided that, regardless of how interesting they were, I wasn't going to read any more books about how to be pregnant; I allowed my body to do exactly what it knew to do, what it was made to do. Watching my baby on the Ultrasound and listening to the heartbeat was both miraculous and enchanting. And labor? I was amazed and humbled at my body's strength.

During my eighteen-hour labor, I soaked in a birthing tub and fell into a light sleep between contractions. I slipped into a dream in which women from every culture and every time period quietly and slowly encircled me, each holding a candle. Their ethereal presence comforted me, sustained me, and gave me strength.

My menses didn't return until six months after my son was born so I didn't bleed for nearly a year and a half. Instead, as if my womb had tossed the baton to my breasts, my body nourished my child through my breast milk.

When my period returned, I was too busy to continue tracking my monthly symptoms, but I knew when I would be fertile. I got pregnant again when I was thirty-nine years old. The doctors considered mine a "risky" pregnancy. I elected not to do the amniocentesis, but an Ultrasound did show abnormalities in my daughter's brain. I had to wait for an excruciatingly long three-day weekend before going in for further testing – which revealed that all was well. Yep, my womb knew, even at the ripe old age of thirty-nine, how to make another healthy baby.

Phase IV. Waning

"I'm here to pick up my prescription," I said, surprised by the catch in my throat.

"Your name?" asked the young woman behind the counter.

"Haggerty."

After riffling through the "H" bin and double checking the computer, she told me that my order would be ready in five minutes.

I wandered over to the waiting area. Looking at my watch, I mentally calculated how long it had been since I had changed my tampon. Two hours. I should be fine until I get home. *How ironic*, I thought, *that I'm picking up a prescription that will take my menses away from me—by sending me into menopause—at the same time that I'm bleeding.* I suddenly became overwhelmed with sadness and my eyes flooded with the waters of grief. I brushed my hand against my cheek to wipe away the overflow, immersed in sorrow. I found myself pacing, trying to catch my breath. Should I be doing this? Am I ready?

I only had three days left of radiation to my right breast. My lumpectomy had been three months prior, and I was spared having to do chemotherapy. Taking Tamoxifen every day for the next five years would reduce my chance of recurrence by half and, given that my chance of recurrence was twenty percent, that was significant. But it would send me into menopause. What was a no-brainer to my doctors, to my husband, to everyone—taking the fucking pill—was a challenging decision for me.

Just like every other woman, I'd been embarrassed by my period; I'd felt shame when I'd leaked through. I'd been overwhelmed by it, especially in the days when I had two toddlers and the days were full of changing diapers, wiping snotty noses, and cleaning their mouths after a meal. I would forget I was bleeding, forget to tend to my own needs, so immersed was I in my children's. I'd been resentful when work meetings ran too long and I knew, I just *knew*, that I needed to get out of there immediately, but couldn't face standing up, not knowing if I'd gushed and leaked through my pants.

I'd never wanted to be ashamed by my body, by this amazing cycle all women go through every month. By now, I'd grown to love the monthly cycle of my body, of my emotions and of my spirit. Through my menses, my body, mind and spirit were linked. I wasn't ready to give that up.

"Ms. Haggerty? Your prescription is ready."

I wiped my cheeks and brushed the snot from my nose as I turned to address the young woman behind the counter. As I pulled out my debit card she asked, "Have you taken this medication before?"

"No," was all I could muster.

"Please wait here for the pharmacist." I looked up at her, she looked at me. It was painfully obvious that I was crying. She quickly turned away.

The pharmacist came over to me, a balding man in his late thirties, and looked at me through his glasses. "Hello," he said as he scanned the bag with my medication. "So you haven't taken this before. Do you have any questions?"

"Ummmm....." *Is there a pill to make this all go away? Can you reverse time so I don't get cancer?...* "No." Tears streamed down my face and I quickly wiped them away.

He looked right at me and said, "Well, you may experience hot flashes. This will likely put you into menopause. Night sweats are common. Of course, the extreme side-effect is uterine cancer, but," he looked up at me again, reassuringly, "that's very rare." The tears didn't stop flowing and he never acknowledged them. When he was finished, I didn't even say thank you. I just walked away.

As I walked toward the exit, I kept my head low to avoid recognizing a neighbor in the store and bee-lined it to the parking lot. I got in my car, threw the medication onto the passenger's seat and started bawling. Guttural, wrenching sobs.

Is this my last period? Will I ever bleed again? Images of my babies flashed before me. The visual montage of women from ages past that I saw during my labor with my son, filled me. *I love my monthly cycle. I don't want it to end. And I really don't want cancer to take* this *away from me, too.*

Phase V.

That was my last period.

It's been nearly five years since I've bled. I think this must be how it feels to live where it's sunny all the time. No seasonal cycles, no drastic weather patterns, just the sun. Yes, there's something lovely about the predictability of not having my monthly menses, but I miss the ebb and the flow, the vitality and volatile cycle of my womb.

Because the floods of my blood have dried up, I'm technically barren. Which makes me remember . . . there is springtime in the desert.

And I hear it's beautiful.

Colleen Haggerty is a writer of memoir and personal essay and has been published in various anthologies. Her memoir, *A Leg to Stand On*, a finalist for the National Indie Excellence Awards, recounts her journey into motherhood as an amputee. An inspirational speaker and coach, Colleen was a speaker at TEDxBellingham, sharing her story of forgiveness.

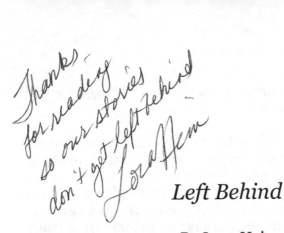

Left Behind

By Lora Hein

I'm wet and cold. Wetter and colder than the last time I woke up. Sleep has relieved me of my awareness. Peggy is motionless underneath me, so I hesitate to move more than an eye blink. Open or closed, my eyes perceive little difference in the darkness, other than when closed they are warmer. The cold follows the wet like a little brother tagging along, unwanted yet unshakable.

I'd give anything right now to have my youngest brother here with me. He's safe at home in San Anselmo, starting his first year of high school, while I, the elder of his two big sisters, have finally graduated from community college, five years after leaving high school. I also have recently achieved the goal he has bragged about to his classmates: "I want to be just like my big sister when I grow up," pause, "a Backcountry Park Ranger." He waits for that to register with his chest puffed out a bit.

Now I am lost on a foreign desert island, too far for him to follow. After taking over three weeks of trains, planes and lucky breaks to get to the Galápagos Islands, within two days of being here, Peggy and I have managed to get lost. Right at this moment I am hoping I will live through this night to see my brother again. Three and a half weeks have passed since I crammed my backpack and daypack into a friend's car with two of my fellow travelers and their gear, plus the driver. We traveled across California to Mexicali to board a train across Mexico for the beginning of our journey to the Galápagos Islands. The day before we left I was at the Army-Navy Surplus Store buying the khaki trousers and shirt I am wearing now. The radio broadcasting music while we shopped was interrupted to announce the Chilean military had ousted Allende in a coup at the Government palace in Santiago. The next day, September 12, 1973, we were on our way to South America.

The green nylon windbreaker zipped over my torso doesn't keep the wicked wet *garua* mists from working through two layers of fabric, no matter how tightly woven to keep wind and bugs out. The damp digs into my pores, dislodging salty sweat and dust from yesterday, or is it still today? It was October 8th when we set out so blithely on our hike up the trail from Puerto Ayora to the highland settlement of Bellavista on our quest to gather as many unripe avocadoes as we could. We needed them to ripen during the month ahead. Our departure was set for 3 a.m. October 9th on the thirty-five foot fishing boat, the *Cristo Rey*, for the next thirty-one days through the archipelago.

Donna, our trip leader, had just finalized arrangements with them to take the eight of us as passengers for a month to visit the islands included in the itinerary she'd planned. Peggy and I had left all our gear with our six companions for them to load onto the boat. We had only met the local fisherman who would captain the boat, Adolpho, and his mate, Sixto, that morning as we left at dawn to beat the lowland heat as we climbed to the highlands.

What time, or which day is it now? I wonder. Neither of us has a watch. Even if either of us were wearing one, we couldn't read it anyway in this mist shrouded equatorial dark.

We've brought none of our usual hiking essentials such as flashlight, matches, compass, or map. Our only map has no more detail than a rough ovoid not much bigger than my thumb, with two concentric squiggly lines marking elevation contours at 300 meter intervals. This island, Santa Cruz, is about three times higher than Mt. Baldy, the foothill to Mt. Tamalpais in the backyard of the house where I grew up. I wonder if I will ever wander the familiar trails of home again. We are completely unprepared to spend the night somewhere on the upper flanks of a volcano 600 miles from the South American continent. Only one extra layer and a quart of water was tucked into each of our empty daypacks in anticipation of our return descent being cooler than the climb.

It's cooler, all right. Chill seeps through both layers of clothes and into my socks at toes and heels; the only dry place is the midsection of wool inside my second-hand leather hiking boots. I bought them so I could leave my good Pivetta Cortina boots at home to protect them from being raked apart by jagged volcanic rocks with edges sharp as broken glass.

My thoughts of volcanic discomfort seem to have penetrated Peggy's dreams. I feel her shift slightly.

"Are you awake?" I whisper, in case she isn't. I don't wish to deprive her of sleep, but I am also hoping she hears me. The old saying 'misery loves company' could not be truer right now. Besides, I am holding back the urge to shiver; if we don't switch places soon I won't be able to avoid shaking her.

"Yeah, I'm feeling bruises forming in new places from the last comfortable-as-I-could-get position. Can we trade again?"

How many times have we gingerly swapped from top to bottom and back since we stopped walking at sundown? At least three, if I haven't lost count. Already becoming routine, the "bottom" rolls to one side to wait while the shivering "top" positions herself as best she can, head resting on avocado stuffed nylon daypacks, hard as round river rocks. We wedge hips, knees, elbows and shoulders into crevices, straddling the pokier points with waist, neck and other softer anatomy. Then, ever so carefully, as if the other were a porcupine, the previous "bottom" lowers onto the other, trying to settle as lightly as down, sheltering and returning warmth gathered since the last turn on top.

Once rearranged and fully awake, I resume speculating where we left off at our previous turning, "Do you think anyone has noticed we're missing yet?"

"If it isn't midnight and the *Ninfa* is still open, Donna, Darran and Ann will still be at the bar."

"But MB, John and Richie could be wondering where we are."

"Unless they went to the boat when it got dark to wait for us and are thinking we may have stopped at the *Ninfa* for something to eat."

Considering that possible scenario, I'm not sure John would think it likely I would be at the bar with Donna instead of getting back to the boat. He's still the only one of the group who knows she told me to go home the last night we were in Guayaquil before boarding the *Floreana* to get to the islands. Even my best friends, Peggy and MB, are not privy to what John overheard. He and I agreed to keep to ourselves Donna's claim that "everyone" wanted me to go home instead of continuing on with the group.

Instead, I reply, "Well, if John, MB and Richie are on the *Cristo Rey* and know we haven't returned, maybe MB or John will insist Richie say something to Adolpho and Sixto, since he has the best grasp of Spanish."

"Richie may not want to incur Donna's wrath."

Even though I've said nothing to Peggy, she has witnessed Donna laying down the law of the trip, telling us all as soon as she'd secured the hiring of two fishermen and their boat, "I'm the only one who speaks with them about any changes to the itinerary. We need a simple chain of command to avoid any confusion."

"And what if Adolpho and Sixto are at the *Ninfa* with the other drinkers, having a last hoorah before heading out into the uninhabited islands with eight Gringos?"

"It is possible John, MB and Richie could be asleep by the time the others return and bed down on the deck without realizing we're not in the bunks below. The crew could pull the anchor and leave Puerto Ayora on the tide at 3:00 a.m. as scheduled."

"If they do, we're sunk. Although, to be accurate, we can't sink if we're not on the boat."

"Do you really think they'd leave us behind? Abandon us?"

"Maybe not on purpose," I respond. "But if they arrive at Floreana Island before everyone else wakes up and notices we aren't on board, do you really think Donna would sacrifice an entire day she's paid for to return to Santa Cruz to try to find us?"

If we aren't worth waiting for, I am guessing the avocados we spent all day searching for and squeezing into our now bulging daypacks aren't worth waiting for either. Feeling less valuable to the others than food feels like the worst possible disregard. Whether my embarrassment or fury are what is making me flush, or the weight of Peggy's slender body is finally driving out the chill, at least wet and cold are not the most pressing sensations any more.

Momentarily relieved of discomfort, Peggy eventually becomes vulnerable to the exhaustion of our arduous day and fades into the reprieve of sleep. Silence surrounds us once more, pervasive as the dense, moist *garua* obscuring the waxing first quarter moon.

A while later, no idea again how much time might have passed in sleep, my discomfort at being stiffly angled over rocks and thorns brings my awareness inevitably back to our predicament. When Peggy starts shivering it is her turn to ask if I'm awake. We switch places again and resume conversation.

Maybe because now her joints are the ones being bruised and bent, she opens with a new twist to our dismal prospects. "Do you know people have disappeared in these islands? Some have never been found. Others' bones might be the ones stumbled upon years after anyone who knew them is still alive."

I have no response. All my reading has been about geology, plants and animals we are looking forward to seeing. I had no idea Peggy has been boning up on the scanty human history of these islands first called "*Las Encantadas*" or "Enchanted Islands." The name derived from the way they mysteriously "disappeared" when cloaked with the *garua* covering us now, sort of like Brigadoon.

The Humboldt Current coming from Antarctica swings out from Peru into the Pacific at the equator. When it bumps into these islands its colder water wells up to the surface. Moisture laden air evaporates as it is warmed and rises over the islands during the day. Then it condenses as the sun goes down and the air cools. A dense cover of mist gathers on the upper slopes of the volcanoes, obscuring the islands, making them appear to be mere clouds. This shroud hovers long into daylight hours during the cooler months of July to December known locally as the "*garua* season."

Hearing no response from me, Peggy continues her morbid line of thought, "A group of sailors stranded on the south coast of Santa Cruz in the 1800s tried to hike into the interior of the island in search of water. The rest of their crew waited for them as long as they could and eventually had to sail away to find another source for the water their shipmates failed to get. Some settlers on the island have discovered human bones that may be all that remained of those sailors."

After a brief pause, again with no response from me, she persists, "Even the earliest parties to officially discover the islands had to chew cactus for moisture, and two men and ten horses died before they could get back to Peru. I imagine their horses weren't too keen on chewing cactus."

"Are you saying you think whether the others leave the island in the morning or do search for us, we could be too lost to make it out of this obscure condition alive?"

"Well, I have been wondering ..." her voice trails off and resumes after several breaths. "At least we're here with each other. We've had some pretty great adventures together. If I have to spend my last days delirious from thirst and hunger or maybe dying of hypothermia from this dreadful *garua*, there are few people I'd rather share my last days with than you."

I let that sink in for a bit. Peggy's right, we've shared some great adventures.

"Remember that New Year's Eve we were both on late shift at Yosemite Lodge?"

"I remember skiing out into El Cap meadow."

"Those big flat snow crystals sparkled in moonlight bright enough to see colors!"

"We've hiked a lot with just moonlight or even starlight. Night in the Sierra sure is different from this deep dark gloom we can't even see each other in, much less find our way anywhere, if we had a clue which direction to go."

"Well, let's hope the mist will clear enough to find our way back to the road tomorrow in the daylight. We won't be able to get far if we can't get our bearings with some visibility." I had been reassured to hear Peggy shift to a more optimistic note. Now we've returned to the gloomy prospect of never finding our way out of here, or at least not finding our way back soon enough.

A few more minutes of quiet contemplation go by. Before I am certain Peggy has dozed again, I reply, "I hope we make it out alive. There are a lot of people I'll miss if we don't. Even so, I'm glad you're the one I'm here with, even if we are the last people we ever see again."

It takes a lot longer for me to fall asleep this time, as I consider my possible mortality. Eventually I doze. When we wake and turn and wake and turn again, we keep discussion to the minimum needed to exchange places. Finally, after the longest twelve hours I have ever known, we are able to see each other, as well as the barbed wire fence we'd followed as the sun plummeted us into darkness the night before—and the mango tree next to our final resting place. That is all we can see in the gray light of early day. I'm grateful to still be alive but concerned to see the fog has not lifted. Standing slow and stiff from our discomfort, we re-shoulder our heavy packs and decide to follow the fence back the way we had come.

We proceed with great caution as well as weariness. Eventually, we pass the brambly place where we first encountered the fence. As we continue, thickets of thorny vines give way to grasses not quite as tall and saw-edged as those we forced our way through the day before, suggesting we aren't precisely retracing our steps. We make slow progress. Then the fence vanishes into dirt. We plop down in wet grass, crestfallen, at a loss of what to do next besides wait until the mist clears enough to reveal landmarks.

As we wait, we plan. If we've not wandered too far from two hummocky knobs we saw the previous afternoon, then our best bet might be to climb toward those landmark bumps to get back to the road. We could then backtrack our route from the day before, back to Bellavista, where we hope we'll find help.

Our vista expands as the mist slowly clears enough to see a few yards farther. In the middle of a shallow depression in the terrain several peculiar rocks appear, very smooth and round about the size of a hassock or truck tire, dark and shiny from moisture. We puzzle over their volcanic history. Then one of them seems to move. We approach closer and notice another moving slowly, then another, at which point we simultaneously plunk down right where we are and dissolve into hysterical laughter.

We have found the fabled tortoises of the island! We knew the road being constructed to connect Puerto Ayora with the northern point across the channel from the airstrip on Baltra Island had been completed beyond Bella Vista, we just did not know how far. Though Donna had stricken the tortoise preserve from our itinerary, we knew it was somewhere near the current end of the pavement.

Now all we need to do is head uphill until we reach the road, turn right, and retrace steps that will lead us back to the harbor, the *Cristo Rey* and our friends, if they are still there. And if they are not? At least this adventure is less likely to cost us our lives than we feared in our misery the night before.

We don't tarry to watch the tortoises, but instead trudge

upwards, the morning mists lifting, revealing the two knobby hills we had hoped to see. Once back on smoother pavement, we regain some strength and step along at a determined pace. Soon we hear a motor approach from behind. It is one of two trucks we've heard make trips between highlands and Port providing transport for anyone who needs it.

We need it.

Brown hands reach out and pull us up into the bed of the truck, the cab being filled by a couple of women and children. Hand gestures direct us to seat ourselves with our backs against the rear window of the cab, from where we take stock of our fellow travelers. In addition to the smiling faces of a couple of local farmers, we count several chickens and a trio of goats being taken somewhere we prefer not to think about.

Thus, as we jostle along the bumpy road, we notice the one other truck on the island passing us. We see John and Richie peering out around the sides at our truck as they speed past. Unfortunately, the people and animals crowded between hide us from their view. The other small white vehicle recedes into the distance leaving us both relieved and chagrined, knowing they are looking for us and therefore have not sailed away on the boat. But we are in the truck heading back from whence they have come, and we have no way to let them know.

At last we arrive at the dusty intersection of the road to the highlands and the spur to shops, campground and research station. With many "muchas gracias's," we stumble from the truck and stagger directly to the dock in hopes of finding friends and food. The *Cristo Rey* is still at anchor. MB's face over the railing opens into the widest grin I have ever seen from her thin lips. Her eyes behind her wire-rimmed glasses sparkle with relief that we are all right. She explains they realized something had gone awry the evening before and alerted the skipper, Adolpho, and his crew not to leave as planned. That morning John and Richie decided they would catch a ride to the highlands to look for us, while the other three, disgruntled their adventure had not begun as planned, arranged to borrow horses to go riding, with the excuse they might come across us.

We are relieved when John and Richie arrive just as we are about to devour the lunch MB has prepared. They came to see if we were back, since their search had proved fruitless. Later we learn one impediment to them finding us was no one had seen two women anywhere. Those they spoke with reported seeing a lady and a man, but not two women. Apparently, my khaki shirt and pants, coupled with my short hair, had led the locals to take me for a man. Peggy established her true gender with her flowered blouse.

A little later, the horseback riding threesome returns and our motley crew can be on our way at last. Donna may not like it, but we're on this boat together after all.

Lora Hein, inspired by her Galápagos experiences, applied her awareness of nature to many endeavors: studying air pollution effects, designing sustainable buildings, teaching elementary school, and serving as a National Park Ranger-Naturalist. She recently returned to writing about her formative Galápagos experiences. She lives in Washington, within sight and smell of saltwater.

Arriving

By Anneliese Kamola

I. Am. In. Amsterdam. Holy crap! I don't feel like I know any thing except that my name is Anneliese Kamola, I'm 24 years old, and I'm sitting on the ground with my small gray hiking backpack as my only companion. I have no idea where I am in the city, what time it is, or even where I'm going to sleep tonight. I have a day's worth of food in my bag. I'm sitting under some kind of tree I don't recognize, on a small strip of grass beside a canal that smells fresh—even though the water is brown—near three brightly painted houseboats and a bridge. The breeze is like a clean piece of parchment paper. The colors of the trees along the cobblestone street are green, light green, and white. I am jetlagged, and everything looks fuzzy.

This is fucking perfect.

A man with long gray hair and strong calves rides by on a humming bicycle, tulips overflowing from the front basket. He whistles as he pedals! Lovely. There is a lady on a houseboat to my right, eating green apples and golden cheese in the sunshine. She's wearing a black and white striped dress. Two kids are in the boat behind her. All are barefoot.

I'm chomping on a still-mostly-firm cucumber, a hard-boiled egg, and some nut-chocolate trail mix—fiber, hydration, protein, salt, and crunch, the finest combination of travel food. I anticipated feeling terrified in a new country away from everything that I know, but, instead, I feel content all the way into my bones.

Last night feels like a different lifetime.

I practically hid in Vicki's postage-stamp-sized New York City apartment. A swarm of overactive worries about my first solo overseas travel kept me pinned to her couch. Vicki made me a salad of romaine greens, chicken, mandarin oranges, almonds, and a creamy poppy seed salad dressing. I could hear cars honking incessantly out the window. People shouting in response. I wanted them to all chill out, go home, go to bed, and give me some peace.

Vicki handed me the bowl. "You sure you don't want to go out there? You came all this way and you don't even want to go check out the city?"

"No way, Vicki, I'm exhausted and I haven't even started my trip. I'm so freakin' scared. Oh God," I paused. "I don't know if I can even eat."

"Girlfriend, you gotta eat," Vicki said as she sat down on the arm of the sofa across from me, holding her own bowl of salad. She lasered me with coal-dark eyes. "What are you so scared about?"

"I have no idea what the frick I'm doing, Vic. I'm just, I don't know. Following my gut. I feel *crazy*." She raised an eyebrow, as if to say, *Go on?* "Yeah. Crazy. God—Dad and I had another fight last night. It was a train wreck. I was packing my bags and was feeling super overwhelmed and just went downstairs for a break and he started asking questions. I was trying to tell him how scared I felt, and he just started laying into me out of nowhere. Where are you going and what are you going to do and what do you mean you don't have a plan? Jeez, I mean, I'm figuring it out as I go along! He already knew that. I told him before. I tried answering his questions in a logical way, but he just got madder and madder, making his German '*Doch*' noise and eye-rolling at anything I said. He basically made a case that I'm not prepared or responsible or whatever for this trip, and that if anything happens, quote: 'Don't Come To Your Mother Or Me If You Need Anything Because We're Not Going To Help You.' What the fuck was that about?"

Vicki looked nonplussed. "What did you say back?"

"I just said, 'Fine. I hear you loud and clear. I won't ask.' I got all cold and clammed up like always—*damn it*—and went upstairs to pace around and rage quietly on my own. As I do." I sighed, mad at myself for not knowing how to communicate with my father.

"I think he's just scared for you," Vicki said, skewering a mandarin orange slice onto her fork. She had always been matter-of-fact. I looked at her, sitting on the arm of the couch, legs crossed, focusing now on her salad. Her black hair was meticulously braided into small cornrows like a crown, and her mahogany skin gleamed in the fading evening light.

Vicki was as close to a sister as I'd ever had, even though our heritages were from opposite hemispheres. Whereas she was dark-skinned and lean, athletic and classically elegant, I was curvier—even a bit too round—slightly awkward, and white as white could be, except when I get sunburned and resemble a lobster.

Five years prior we met as high-school freshman in the Intro to Drama class. Her resonant voice, powerful presence, and penchant for hysterical one-liners immediately mesmerized me. Over the next four years we acted across from each other in a number of plays; our sisterhood ran through many storylines, not only our own.

"What makes you so sure it's fear, Vicki?"

"Of course he's scared." She looked at me and smiled. "You quit your job. You've been living on someone's glassed-in front porch for three months through the winter. You're spending your last pennies to travel overseas. You don't have a plan and you only have one tiny backpack. You're single, young, and a woman. Your life could sound ridiculous to anyone."

God, I thought. She's so blunt. "But Vic, I've just got to *go*," I said, looking down at my folded hands, starting to feel frustrated that I had to defend myself with my friend.

"Oh, I know. Don't worry, I get it. This story you're starting with? It's important. I mean, *really important*. Who else our age really *knows* about the Holocaust? I don't. Not the way you do. It was—what?—two weeks in world history class and reading *Diary of Anne Frank* for extra-credit in ninth grade? That's not much. And besides, Anni. I know you. You're an artist through-and-through. It's your *soul's job* to make things magically work out of nothing." Her approval made me smile. I still didn't quite trust that my driving compulsion to create made me an artist, but I enjoyed being seen in this light.

My sister-friend had attended one of the best theater schools in the country, and after graduating she moved to New York City to try her hand at professional acting. To me, moving to a giant city to base one's finances on theater was a way larger risk than traveling overseas to the tiny town of Coburg to land on the couch of my parents' friends.

I traced my fingers on the seams of Vicki's leather sofa.

"Hey, Anni," she said, her voice low and soft. I looked up at her. "You're gonna be fine. This art we do? It's just God. It's just God talking. You know this. We're just God-made vessels, big gorgeous-woman vessels. And the creativity that moves through us makes us all...all sparkles and wow. Right now, this trip is your canvas." She had balanced her salad on her lap and was moving her hands theatrically in curves and flares, her long fingers flipping all the way to the tips of her nails. She leaned forward and looked directly at me, her eyes wide. "We just gotta shut up and do it, you know?" She leaned back, picked up her salad again, and stabbed some lettuce onto her fork. "Girrrrrl, you gonna be fine out there."

I smiled, exhaled, and nodded. Then picked up my salad bowl.

As I crunch the last bite of the emerald green cucumber, 3,700 miles away from Vicki's couch, I can't help but grin thinking about her. We share something *alive*. A kind of feeling. Young twenties, just out of college. A sense that anything is possible—because it *is*. Obama was elected three years ago, on the power of youth. *Hope* was a word that he—and we—ran on.

The night of his election, parades spontaneously erupted across the United States. In downtown Bellingham, Washington, where I went to college, people rushed the streets wearing costumes and beads, carrying flags. A flash-mob of Michael Jackson's *Thriller* pranced down Railroad Avenue to music booming over speakers, a repeat of the Halloween performance from four nights before. The noise of car horns, yelling, cheering, bottles breaking, and drunken college students flowed by my house for hours. My three housemates and I shared a little celebration of our own, making quesadillas and drinking cheap red wine in our drafty kitchen.

"Oh my God, I can't *believe* it!" I said, plopping down next to Sarah on the couch in the kitchen. Electricity ran through my body. I felt giddy, like I could have hugged the moon. "He *won!*" A president so young, so grounded. A man who had somehow *mobilized so many youth with a message of positivity.* If he could do this, what could the rest of us do? Barak Obama emanated a different kind of hope than other presidents. He wasn't an ancient talking-head; even though he was almost 50, I could relate to his gigantic smile, his youthful energy, his active body, and his obvious excitement for the future. To me, his message held power. Possibility. "I think I'm still in shock."

"Yea!" grinned Hunter. My lanky six-foot-five housemate leaned against the counter, holding his plate with one hand and folding his quesadilla in half with his other as he prepared to scarf it down. "Man, it's all so great!" he said taking a giant bite. "Did you see all the photos online of people partying all over the country? It's craaa-zy!" Hunter spoke through chewing, and shook his surfer-boy hair out of his eyes.

"I don't know," said Cameron as he stood at the stove. Shorter and stockier than Hunter, Cameron's demeanor was that of an intellectual, stubborn bull. "Obama's just another politician."

"Oh, come on, Cameron," Sarah chided him, swirling her wine.

"He's a great person," Cameron said, "I don't doubt it. But you have to remember that he's working in a system that's larger than him. Totally ruthless. His promises are like promising extra recess time when running for class president in middle school."

"Cameron, can'tcha just lighten up and celebrate while we have cause to?" Sarah asked.

"I'll celebrate when something actually happens," he countered.

"When something happens? A black man was just elected president!" Sarah half-yelled, half-laughed out of amazement. "C'mon, Cameron. You can't deny that this is history. Right here."

"It's more'n history," I added, pausing between bites. "The narrative of the country is changing. That means our *psyches* are changing. I mean, look at it. We're seeing a new dominant paradigm being written, you know? That's cool."

"But dominant paradigms don't change overnight with one election," said Cameron, switching off the stove. "And it's not just up to Obama. It's up to a whole bunch of people to actually do the work; our world's a mess and there's a lot to be done. So, I'll celebrate when we actually see some concrete changes."

Cameron had irritated me that night, dampening the flames of my excitement with his level-headed practicality. Part of me saw his logic, but I wanted to feel the palpability of change away from corporate domination and the resulting social injustices. I wanted to harness the energy of the election and use it to feed my own growing confidence. I wanted to sit with friends who said yes.

Over the next two years, I kept saying yes in my own life. I said yes to the challenge of self-designing an interdisciplinary major. I said yes to working multiple jobs at once, selling much of my stuff, and living on my friend's front porch from January through March, snuggled under puffy white down comforters, in order to save almost enough money for this trip. I had said yes to invitations from my parents' friends, distant family members, and friends-of-friends in Europe, all whom I have yet to meet.

And now sitting under a tree in Amsterdam, I feel the same pounding yes inside me. This time I am saying yes to moments of potential in myself; yes to risk, homesickness, and fear; yes to strangers; yes to the whims and insanity that, when finally all stacked together, will create the heat of art for my life. I am saying yes to the idea of following my family lineage as far back as I can find: Germany, Poland, Sweden, and Norway. I am saying yes in response to the myriads of dreams and spiritual clues leading me on this trip through Europe. And saying yes has brought me to this very idyllic makeshift picnic spot underneath a blooming mystery tree. I lean back, close my eyes, smile, and rest in the sunshine for a well-deserved moment of stillness.

Shit! I fling my eyes open and hastily pull my backpack over to me. I slip my leg through the shoulder straps and pull my pack all the way up to my hip. I can't believe I didn't do that sooner; thank goodness no one stole her. I lean back against the tree again, thinking about that morning when she was taken from me, at security in the Reykjavik airport.

I had felt tiny, exposed, and vulnerable as I stood empty-handed, watching the guards pull my entire life into public and splay it across a white plastic table. Why did they choose me? What were they looking for? When they let me re-Tetris my bag, I felt agitated.

As I hoisted her onto my back and joined the Customs line, questions flooded my mind. Had the government flagged me for some reason? Would I have to answer questions? Would the Icelandic guard speak English? My bladder threatened to burst.

When I came to the front of the line, a middle-aged officer sitting on a tall stool behind a desk in a plexiglass-encased kiosk waved me forward. His gray-blue cap fit close to his shaved head, and a thin black tie clipped to his shirt. Spectacles. Thin lips. Shoulders muscular and strong. I walked up to the counter and handed him my ticket, passport, and return flight confirmation papers. I had to look up to make eye-contact; the positioning made me feel like a child. My hands shook.

"Hello."

He just nodded in response, and took his time peering over my ticket and paperwork. He paused, then looked down at me, piercing me with ice-blue eyes.

"Sorry. We're going to have to send you back."

I froze. I stared at him. I'm sure my eyes were wide and my face slack in disbelief.

"You can't," I blurted.

"I can't?" He micro-adjusted his head to the left in annoyance.

"You can't. That can't happen." I regrouped. "What's wrong?"

"This ticket is for four months out. You can only be in Europe for three."

How had I missed that detail? That very morning, because I hadn't been able to sleep from nerves, I turned on Vicki's laptop to double-check the Customs rules. *One last time. Just in case.* The room was dark in the pre-dawn, and the blue light from the screen poured over my hands as I scrolled through the governmental page again.

And there, typed immediately after a bullet point, I read that all people traveling with passports, but without Visas, were required upon entry to have a ticket out of the Schengen States — the countries participating in Euro.

"What?" I hissed aloud, the last letter crisp on my tongue. I had prepared for eight months, looked at this page a dozen times, and had not noticed this detail. Everyone I had interviewed about their travels in Europe said they had bought a one-way ticket. But, then again, most of them had traveled a decade earlier. Apparently, times had changed.

"Shit," I admonished myself as I stared at the computer screen. I grabbed my wallet, fished out my bank card, and, with adrenaline pulsing through my body, hurriedly searched the internet for another one-way ticket from Somewhere, Europe to Somewhere, United States.

My idea had been to follow my intuition, my gut, my feet, and the circumstances as they unfolded in my travels. To follow as an act of listening. To say yes, over and over. Maybe even staying in Germany for a year, finding an apartment and a job. How could I follow the yesses if I was forced to put an end date on my dreams?

But laws are laws. I found a fairly cheap ticket from Frankfurt, Germany to New York City for mid-August and—with a steadying breath—paid for it.

"Well, there goes $500.00," I thought to myself.

I printed the confirmation from Vicki's printer, the page whirring out as the daylight started edging in through the window. I folded the slightly warm sheet of paper three times and tucked it into my money belt, only to hand it to the Icelandic Customs Officer ten travel-weary hours later.

"I'm so sorry, Sir. I didn't know that." My voice wobbled. Would he really send me back? What a lot of wasted time and money. I would return completely humiliated. My Dad's sentiment rang in my ears—I was young and inexperienced and foolish.

I gritted my teeth. *I'm not.* I told myself. *I just do things differently. Why can't you understand me?*

"What are you doing in Europe?" the Customs Officer asked.

"Um. Visiting family friends. In, um, Coburg, Germany. It's in Bavaria." Did he think I was making it up and trafficking drugs or something?

"How do you know them?"

"Wolfgang worked for my father in the United States a long time ago." Or something like that. I couldn't quite remember. I made a mental note to ask Wolfgang when I arrived.

The guard searched my face. I'm sure he saw a girl just barely a woman, wearing a new, olive-drab travel cap, a lemon yellow and royal blue shawl over a butter yellow cashmere sweater, comfy jeans and hiking boots, wearing a small gray backpack. Tight face. Body standing tall with pride and willingness. I wondered if he saw vulnerability or strength.

The officer sighed. "Ok. I'll stamp it. But change your ticket *immediately* when you get to Coburg. If it is not changed and you do not leave within 90 days, when you do finally leave the Schengen States, we will track that it has been too long, and you will not be able to return. Ever." His stamp made a dull thud as it landed on the paper, and the wet ink made a slight *ssshik* as he pulled his hand away. He handed the papers back to me.

"Enjoy your travels."

"Yes, Sir. Thank you, Sir. I will, Sir. Oh. Thank you, Sir." I grabbed the paperwork and fled the kiosk so as to not annoy him any further. I walked down the long airport hallway towards my next plane exhaling with relief and thinking a single word: *Ohmygod!Ohmygod!Ohmygod!Ohmygod!Ohmygod!*

"Oh God!" I squawk as a bicycle whizzes by, almost on top of me. A young woman with a thick straw-colored braid swinging down her back is already ten feet away; her amber skirt billows around her legs. If my foot had been out any further, she would have squished my toes. I am already learning valuable travel lessons about where to leave—and not leave—my appendages.

I extricate my leg from my backpack straps, stand, and stretch. The sun is slipping behind the buildings, and the woman on the houseboat dons a lightweight red sweater. I brush the crumbs off of my shirt, then heft my backpack onto my knee, slide it around to my back, hike it above my hips, and clip the weight in across my hips and chest. This series of movements already feels familiar.

I fish a little map out of my pocket. I snagged it from a pile of free maps at a 'Welcome to Amsterdam' airport kiosk earlier in the afternoon. I unfold it and gaze at a labyrinth of streets and canals. A dozen little yellow stars mark the locations of hostels throughout the city.

"Time to find a place to sleep for tonight," I say to a passing pigeon, and turn to follow the cobblestones into the deepening dusk of yes.

Anneliese Kamola, author and developmental editor, lives in Bellingham, WA. She has written, produced, and performed three solo storytelling-theater shows, and is currently writing two books, one about her grandparent's remarkable meeting in WWII Germany, and the second is a coming-of-age story for the current American teen.

A Ride Between Worlds

By Ellen Key

Mother, *I know you might want to leave when there is no one here with you.* "So, I'm going to go ahead and leave the room right now, just in case you do." My hunch was that she didn't want to trouble any of us by making us watch her take her last breath. I walked, slowly and deliberately, to the door of her apartment, and opened it to leave.

"Ewwen! Ewwen!" she called out in a twisted voice. I hardly recognized "Ellen," my own name.

"Okay, Mother, I hear you. I will stay." I stepped back inside the apartment.

She wanted me to be there with her. If this is where she wanted me, I knew she wouldn't slip away during the night, wouldn't let me miss her leave-taking whenever I briefly stepped out for a break during the day.

I had been staying in room number 15 of the Motel 6 for the last week while here in College Station, Texas. I'd already made one trip down from the Dallas area, on October 22nd, the fourth anniversary of Charlie's death. I had felt a familiar "nudging" from him that I needed to go down to see Mother. I had stayed for three days and then returned home, sick. As an empath, I had grown burdened beyond what I could manage by my mother's physical and emotional pain. I'd driven back home to see my family doctor for medical treatment.

But a few days later, unable to be away from her as she lay dying, I drove back down to be with her again. I spent each day, from about 11:00 a.m. until 11:00 p.m., in her little apartment at the assisted living facility and then returned to my motel room at night for rest, to journal and practice self-care. My sister Norma, the baby of six and the only other girl besides me, had also driven down from near Dallas and was sleeping in Mother's assisted living apartment. "Until Mother dies," she said. Our youngest brother, Fred, also came down from the Dallas area and stayed most of the last week. Our oldest brother, Lynn, lived in College Station and as time allowed between teaching assignments, was in and out to visit Mother.

My heart was breaking. While I was there, she rested quietly as I sat and read by her side, sometimes alone and other times, not. My sister restlessly surfed the Internet for information on new drugs our mom was being given. She posted messages via email to family members; her agitation was palpable. Some nights after I left, Norma texted me to report that Mother had become restless and that she tossed and moaned. The hospice nurse told me that although she was unable to speak, our mom was very aware of the energy of each one of her children who entered the room, and that her vitals responded accordingly.

And then, just as with Charlie, just as I had been told by intuitive friends would be the case, it would be me who was going to be there at the end. I "knew" that Time would bend for me to be there, to allow her to use my acceptance and loving presence as a bridge to cross over, when she made her final transition. And I was not afraid of what was to come. Death no longer frightened me.

On Mother's last day, my sister was upset that she had been given more drugs. Her grief was different than mine—it wanted things to be just so for Mother. But things were not just so. Norma grew angry and packed up her duffel bag in tight-lipped silence. Eventually she decided she needed some space and exited the room. I was the one left sitting there by Mother. As I waited for the return of the hospice nurse, I quietly picked up the phone to call my best friend back in Dallas for support. After a minute or so of quiet conversation, I suddenly turned to look over at Mother and saw that she had taken her last breath and made her transition, ever so quietly, while I had been distracted.

So, on November 7, 2016, Mother's seven-month stay at the facility was over. At 5:25 p.m.

Tired and grateful to be with her in her crossover moment, I waited for the mortuary personnel to come and remove my mother's body from the room. My oldest brother, his wife and his son were here now. Along with my sister who had returned. We awkwardly stood around in the wake of her passing, old family wounds and misunderstandings hovering in the air as they do during major events. She was gone and we were left with each other.

Now, I found myself a passenger in an old red pickup truck. Charlie drove and we were jostling up and down, thrown from side to side without seat belts, as we moved along a bumpy dirt road. I had no idea how old this faded red vehicle was. It had rounded front fenders and, turning to look through the back window, I could see the short step-side bed in the back. I bounced high in my seat, before coming down hard on the springs as we hit a pothole in the washboard road.

But, the engine seemed to be running good enough. Like an old workhorse with scars on his flanks from having tangled with a barbed wire fence, he had jutting hip bones that showed his age. It was only a good heart that made him still able to forge ahead to the task asked of him.

A few more scratches were added to the right front fender from close contact with the mesquite bushes as we careened around a corner too closely. I could smell the nearby river. I tasted damp sand in the back of my throat with each breath. Cotton from the cottonwood trees growing down in the Bosque floated through the open windows of the cab. My fingers were cramped from holding onto the edges of the crusted old leather seat. I peered through a jagged crack that ran sideways through my half of the windshield.

Daylight was drawing near, with the sky slowly beginning to change from deep indigo blue to something a little more violet. With not quite enough light to allow one to fully distinguish trees or houses from coyotes running away from us, we drove madly on. Headlights reflecting off of eyes as they turned to look at us told us we had company that night. It mattered not. We were on a mission and time was of the essence.

As we passed a small adobe dwelling with a faint yellow glow coming from a curtained kitchen window, I realized that we were heading the wrong way.

"Turn around! Turn around!" I yelled over the sound of the old engine. "We must have missed the turn!" I flung the words toward Charlie as I peered through the thick dust that settled over us. He slammed on the brakes and the old truck shuddered to a stop.

"Charlie, we need to go back that other way!" I coughed and waved my hand back in the direction we had just come from.

"What?" he looked at me like I had lost my mind, but he turned the old pickup into the nearest dirt driveway and reversed, grinding gears as he did so. Clods of dirt and pieces of buffalo grass and roots flew into the air from the friction between the ground and the tires.

It had been years since Charlie had driven a stick shift, and this old pickup without power steering was hard on him. It made me think of the decrepit red Jeep our dad used to own when we were teenagers. There had been a hole in the floorboard on the passenger's side that allowed you to see the dirt road whizzing by, too close for comfort, beneath your feet. The stick shift sat squarely between the two ratty front seats, but there was no back seat - just a flat metal surface that gave you nothing to hold onto, should you find yourself riding back there. Perhaps this was a sad reincarnation of that Jeep.

Charlie was driving, as my mother would have said, "like a bat out of hell," and we were on our way somewhere important. I felt like we had gone back into time, and outside, the eerie night added to a confused feeling that clutched at my gut.

Had we perhaps really stepped back into time? Or, into a place where Time was standing still? Was it waiting for us before moving onward? All I knew was that I had a sense of urgency ringing in my ears like a bell tolling, telling me that time was running out. I had sweat running down the side of my face, and I wiped it away with one hand, while still clinging to the seat with the other.

As we reversed our course down the dirt road, I saw that the sky was getting lighter and lighter. The sense of being late rushed over me, and I felt a sinking sensation in my stomach.

"It's got to be here, somewhere..." I muttered to myself, as I hung my head out the open window, trying not to get sideswiped by an overhanging cottonwood branch. I peered at the small adobe houses and other buildings that we were hurtling past, with billowing dust clouds on the road behind us.

All of a sudden, a larger building loomed up on the left side of the road. There was a lot of activity there, with vehicles driving in and out of the parking lot. Old beat-up vehicles. Models I hadn't seen since I was a kid. The kind of cars and trucks that older people bought and restored because it reminded them of the time when they were teenagers, back when gas was twenty-four cents per gallon.

Finding a spot on the outer edges of the parking lot, Charlie pulled "Ole Red" into it, and shut off the engine. Why had that name come so easily to my mind? How did I know the name of this old truck?

We got out, and I grabbed Charlie's arm as we headed across the parking lot. His blue plaid shirt was frayed and old, as were his jeans, and his boots looked like he had hiked miles through the mud. Wouldn't have been here in the dry sand hills of the high desert of New Mexico. I looked down at my own clothes. I was dressed in an old favorite peach colored shirt, jeans, and the suede Chucka boots like the ones I'd worn back when I was a teenager. They were great protection to keep from stepping on goat head stickers.

As we reached the front doors of the building, we joined a mass of people entering and had to push our way through the same doorway against people who were exiting. Some of those leaving had a look of sadness you could tell was not going away anytime soon. Others had a shining light in their eyes that was so bright you had to turn away quickly, lest they felt you intruding on private thoughts.

Inside, the hallways were narrow and tight. As we continued to push our way forward, I lost track of Charlie in the crowd of people. The noise was a dull roar that got louder, as you passed by different entryways to additional corridors. I caught a glimpse or two through these and they seemed like they were lit with a golden light. I could see what looked like airplanes pulled up on the tarmac in the distance. There was no one I recognized, and now, I had lost Charlie. Oddly, I did not feel any panic. And that, in itself, stopped me in my tracks. I usually didn't like going places where I didn't know anyone. I did not like being lost with no one else to guide me or help me find my way.

But, I had a knowing from deep in my belly that I was not lost. I was on my way to find someone. Yes, that was it! And I would know when I had found them. Or when they found me... My only task was to keep walking and searching through the crowds. This was a meeting that I was destined to make and I would get there on time.

I just had to trust that everything would become clear in the right time. Trust. Something that I had struggled with all of my life. I always wanted to know where we were headed and what was going to happen when we got there. On family vacations, I had been the navigator, with the map open on my lap, and calculating the miles we drove between gas stations.

In my life, I was the proverbial Girl Scout—always trying to prepare myself for whatever possibility might arise. Like a trial run or a dress rehearsal. This sudden willingness to trust was different.

All of a sudden, I collided with a young woman in her early thirties. About my height, with curly dark brown hair and a tendril that curled down over her right cheek, she was dressed all in white. As soon as I saw her, I reached out to hug her to me in a bear hug. My arms wrapped around her and I held on, as though my life depended on it. And she hugged me just as tightly back. We stood there for a moment frozen in time. I knew I'd never forget that hug. As I stepped back to look more closely at her, I recognized her Soul. She was my mother. Tears began to pour down my face.

With a sudden start, I woke up and realized I was in room number 15 at the Motel 6. I knew I hadn't been dreaming though, not exactly. As I rolled over and reached to turn the digital clock toward me, I felt a deep knowing coming over me that my brother, Charlie, who had crossed over almost exactly four years earlier, had come to me as my driver and guide. We had been on a final rendezvous to meet in Spirit form with my mother's Soul. Tears began pouring down my face. Soon I wept with deep sobs that wracked my body. The sheets were rumpled and finally, I pushed myself back up against the soggy pillow to a sitting position. It was 4:42 a.m., and I had been back in the motel room for about three hours. I'd been lying in the large king-sized bed with an orange wall stretching out behind me, but really I'd been with my beloveds.

I'd been offered a gift from both my brother and mother. He guided me to her, so that she and I could say farewell in a deeply significant way before her Soul moved onward to meet her Spirit Guide and reconnect with her Soul Family on the other side. I knew I would always cherish and often relive that moment. In life, sometimes my relationships with both Charlie and Mother had been difficult, but I saw that Soul to Soul, all was well. I could let go and move on in peace.

Ellen Keys wrote her piece based on her developing memoir, *Conversations with Charlie*. These conversations began right after her brother, Charlie, died unexpectedly in 2012. Ellen was also present, in 2016, for her mother's final moments. She wants others to know that communication with loved ones does not stop at death.

Priceless

By Ann Kremer

The sun seldom poked its bright rays of light from behind the clouds, maybe once or twice as my 17-year-old son Jon and I sat on the black wrought iron chairs placed on the wraparound patio outside the cafeteria that late afternoon. The temperature was still hot into the 90's, so the overcast sky brought little sense of relief. Desert hills extended beyond our view and captivated me in an appreciation of a wilderness different from our own back in Washington State. On the southern horizon, darker clouds moved in on us; the question of whether or not it was going to rain was gone, and now a dim glow of orange took over the sky that made the hair on my arms stand up.

Jon and I glanced at each other and Jon beamed but for a moment. Then a drop, and another, and another. Each the size of a half dollar onto the concrete. Down from above, plup, plup, plup.

"It's polka dot," I said with amusement and a nudge to Jon's arm. The pattern playing at our feet was a simple delight for me in an otherwise somber situation. Buckets of rain came next, and we were forced to scooch the chairs closer to the building next to the glass window and under the awning. I fancied the idea being in the rain and yet able to remain dry.

"Oh my gosh, look at this."

"It's beautiful," he said in weary tone. I understood his weariness. Jon was dressed in pale green scrubs, his socks were from home and his hair was disheveled from lack of being combed. Earlier that day, we had arrived, from Seattle, at the University of Neuroscience Institute on the campus of the University of Utah in Salt Lake City. Jon had been admitted to the adolescent psychiatric unit where I had just been allowed to take him down to the cafeteria. Seattle Children's Hospital in-patient behavioral medicine unit had transferred him here to UNI (they pronounced it "you-nee") because Jon had run through the medical trials at Children's without benefit. He'd been through many different therapies and yet remained sui-cidal and depressed, so we'd agreed to come to UNI for electro-convulsive therapy, a therapy not available at Seattle Chil-dren's—and one I was not enthusiastic about, even though it provided a ray of hope.

"If it can help, then I want to try it," he'd said. He spoke so frankly about dying and how he wasn't afraid to die that I felt forced to hope in this rather extreme treatment measure. He was scheduled for his first ECT treatment the next morning.

I shifted myself as my bottom was becoming uncomforta-ble against the wrought iron seat. I wished this moment of still-ness and relative sanity could last.

"It is really beautiful," I said. The rain slowed down to a drizzle and the heavy, dark clouds moved on passed us like they were on a grand stage, exiting over the grassy hills on the other side. I felt elevated for a few moments above our problems, as if what we just experienced was brought to me and Jon from Mother Nature herself as a sign that his sickness could be washed away. The sun came out and shined through the linger-ing raindrops and produced a full spectrum rainbow right in front of us. The air was clean and fresh with the strong scent of desert sage.

"That was amazing," Jon said as I nodded my head in agreement. "Ya know, Mom, there is something I didn't tell you." He crossed his legs and fiddled with a red shoe lace.

"Yeah? Go ahead." I turned my body toward him. I had no idea what he was about to share, but I'd learned to be ready for anything, so I kept my breathing calm and my face receptive.

"At night after you'd go to sleep, I often took the car out. I'd go to that beach over by Amanda's."

"Dockton?"

"Yes, that one," he replied. "And I'd cut." He paused for a moment to check my reaction. I gave him none. This hadn't al-ways been the case. There had been many, many times, before I'd grown tired and traumatized, that I wasn't able to stay calm and had reacted dramatically to news of self-harm.

"I see."

"It was my only relief. I would look forward to it all day." His voice pleaded for validation, not that it is an all right thing to do, but rather that he was being heard. My stomach ached badly as I took in what my son had just said. It wasn't so much the fact that he'd been self-harming that caused my ache at the moment—I'd known about this behavior for quite some time—but rather the additional reason to distrust his judgment. He'd been taking my car in the middle of the night. On the island, the roads are very curvy and narrow, and there are no street lights except in the small business districts. A deer could have jumped out in front of him without any warning. Or another car speeding the opposite direction, perhaps thinking no one else is on the road so late at night, could have cut corners short by moving into the other lane.

The cutting itself is such a mystery to me. How did he manage that without blood landing on the upholstery? Maybe he sat out on the picnic table and sliced himself up as the moon shined on the water? He liked his scars. The fact that he enjoyed cutting made my skin crawl. I tried to understand its meaning for him, but I struggled with it; I only saw the bleeding lacerations that I bandaged, the healing wounds, or residual scars. He said it eased the intensity and depth of his inner pain and sometimes has kept him alive.

"Thanks for telling me," I replied. "And don't ever take the car without my knowing again,"

"Ok, I know and I'm sorry I did that," he said.

I wondered what else he had in his back pocket that he's not telling me.

The bright colors of the rainbow stretched from the hillside to the desert hills in front of us.

"It's magical," I said in awe as I contemplated how nature can provoke one's truth. We stood to go back into the building. I caught the door into the cafeteria where the sound of dishes clanking meant they would soon serve dinner. We decided it would be best he get back upstairs so he wouldn't miss the food. Outside the unit door, I buzzed the button on the wall for the staff inside.

"Hi. Your code please?" a voice responded.

"8282," I said, then a click to the door let us in.

Inside, there were glass enclosed meeting rooms along the short hallway toward the unit. Jon and I had met with a psychiatrist earlier that day in the second room on the left. We'd sat there with the small plain sofa, low coffee table, and two upholstered chairs. The room was small but had a large window that displayed the facility's expansive view of the Salt Lake valley and Wasatch Mountains. We had been escorted by the front desk staff to the room after we arrived from the airport to UNI. Jon had run his fingers through his hair as he looked about before sitting down on the sofa against the wall and setting his black backpack next to him. For a moment, I couldn't decide where I should sit, as if it really mattered. I gave up and just took the chair across from Jon. My hands were damp, my heart beat a quickly, and what felt like fuel ran in my veins. Dr. Peters entered after a few long moments and welcomed us to Salt Lake. He introduced himself and went back to close the door. He had a relaxed step as he made his way to the chair under the window which sat between Jon and me.

"ECT is 80% effective," he said, jumping right into explanation.

I truly hope so, I thought.

"It is used when people don't respond to oral antidepressants and or have had multiple suicide attempts."

I made note he was handsome. Mid-forties, dark haired, clean shaven, dressed in dark suit with matching tie. His presentation felt sincere, yet I could tell he'd done this a hundred times.

"We have the records from Seattle Children's Hospital regarding the suicide attempts," he continued, "treatment you've had for depression and social anxiety and you've been through Dialectic Behavior Therapy too, right?"

Jon sat tall with his full attention on the doctor and responded, "Yes."

"Mom, can you tell me a bit about how Jon was growing up?"

"Sure." I said as I straightened myself. "He was an easy baby, easily soothed. Met most of his milestones early. Walked by a year. Had his front four permanent teeth by kindergarten. He was well liked by his teachers and other kids because of his innate empathy for others. He is a good listener and learner. He's more articulate than I am. Got mostly A's in school until around eighth grade when things got tough. That's when he stopped going to school. I regret maybe I didn't see it coming, or failed to respond to him in a way he needed, or I wasn't sensitive enough because he was so well adapted."

"You can't blame yourself," Dr. Peters injected as he rubbed his hands as if washing them. "It is not your fault. People are a combination of genetics, brain chemistry and environment, and how they interpret that is their own. It's not just you."

"I'll take that to heart," I replied in a subdued tone, feeling vulnerable having shared my insecurities. It isn't so easy to convince a mother her child's problems aren't her fault.

"Memory loss is what people worry the most with ECT," Dr. Peters explained. "Jon has tried many modalities of treatment from medication, therapy, and classes and remains stuck in this depression. He has desperately tried to get well. And that he still struggles does not mean these treatments were in vain. ECT is performed at the lowest of lows of depression. The initial treatment is ten to twelve treatments within a three-week period. Then follow up treatments as necessary when needed.

"This will lift your depression, Jon," he said in a kind manner. "I don't see you needing any maintenance treatments, but we'll see. We had an older woman who came back to us after 20 years from her initial treatments. Not until then did she need a maintenance treatment. For others it can be a month or a year. It is better to get a maintenance treatment when you start to spiral down, when just a treatment or two can bring you back up, rather than waiting to hit bottom when a full series of treatments would again be required." He moved his hands swiftly about in front of himself and continued on, "Medication has not been enough. Thirty to forty percent of people get full benefit with medication, while another 30 percent get some improvement and the other 30 percent get no relief from depression with medication."

I found it hard to keep up with all the information he was giving us. I didn't even try to take notes. A pamphlet would sure be nice; I decided to ask if they had one later. My mind was getting hazy. I was going to turn my son over to this guy to electrocute his brain when my own brain didn't even seem able to keep up.

"Do you have any questions?" he asked.

"No," I said impulsively, but then said, "No, yes, I do, what is the memory loss we could see?" Jon was smart. I didn't want his memory or ability to learn compromised.

"There are a lot of negative things said about ECT. Both online and how it has been portrayed in the movies. Most famous being *One Flew Over the Cuckoo's Nest*. Yes, in the 1950s they basically plugged in the machine and turned it on. Now its administration is completely controlled and at much lower doses than back then. Spontaneous seizures affect memory, and so will this.

"Around the 5th, 6th, and 7th treatments you'll have some trouble remembering things from the day before, you may ask the same questions over and over. Treatments 8, 9, and 10, you may have a spacey feeling, catch yourself staring at the wall or the TV. Your head may feel as if it is detached from your body, or you may have a murky feeling or experience deja vu. Most of the time, these treatments are done on an outpatient basis, though, so these side effects don't tend to be serious.

"Around one week after your last treatment, the fog will clear and you'll have an 'oh, yeah' feeling. Around two to four weeks after treatment, you'll be back to your better self. After six months, full memory will have returned except for the period just before and during treatments. That will not return. But most people agree, better to live their lives without depression than to have that piece of memory."

My head was really spinning now. We were about to screw with Jon's sense of reality. I looked at my son and couldn't catch his eye. Did he really want to do this?

"Tell me about the procedure," Jon asked confidently. Apparently he was not as daunted as I was.

"The procedure will only last about 10 minutes. The seizure itself is about 30 to 45 seconds. You can wear your clothes. A blood pressure cuff will be placed on your arm and an oximetry on your finger that tells us your pulse and how well your blood is oxygenated. There will be an anesthesiologist and myself in the room and a nurse. They'll first put you to sleep with some medicine in your IV. You'll also be given a muscle relaxant to stop any movement during the seizure.

"I've done this many, many times and know the exact amount of shock to administer to cause a seizure. Only when the first shock doesn't work, do we bump it up. When it's all over, we let you recover a bit and take you over to the recovery area where you'll wake up. And you'll be wheeling back upstairs in about 30 minutes total."

My gaze slowly sought Jon's. *Well?* I thought.

"I want to do it." Jon looked at Dr. Peters.

Now my eyes moved across the room to the window and out toward the mountains in the distance. Jon would be eighteen in two months. It felt odd it to have him involved in such major medical decisions. Up until now, his father and I had made all the major calls regarding his treatment. This one was up to him. And he'd said yes.

"I'll put you first on the schedule for Monday, that's tomorrow. That means you'll be here at five in the morning. I'm on tomorrow, so I'll be your doctor. Anything else I can answer for you now?"

A brief shake of our heads and we stood.

"Not right now. Thank you," I said and extended my hand to shake his, already extended. Dr. Peters then turned toward Jon and did the same then picked up his brown briefcase to go. I noticed the smoothness of the back and thought, *That's expensive leather*.

We followed him out the door and toward the entrance to the adolescent unit.

"Here, I'll let you in," he said with a quick bobble of his bag. Then he swiped his hospital badge attached to his suit coat on the wall pad, the door buzzed, and Jon and I awkwardly both aimed for the door.

After getting Jon settled in his room and then walking him to the cafeteria, I said, "I'm going to go now."

"Thanks, Mom," he towered over me, but I could see the child I once knew in his eyes. "You'll be here before I go tomorrow, right?"

He was anxious, I could tell, but I'd also heard the determination in his voice when he was talking with the doctor. Should I try to talk him out of this? Shocking the brain seemed beyond extreme. But Jon had been in pain for years and nothing we'd done had helped. He was taking matters into his own hands now. Still, I was his mother. Shouldn't I weigh in?

"Yes. I'll be here before you go in for the treatment. Rest well, I love you." I gave a little wave to the staff behind the circular desk. The receptionist acknowledged my intention to leave with a nod and buzzed the door for me to exit.

When I reached the open stairwell, everything got really quiet. I opened the door to a blast of Salt Lake City heat. My rental car was parked near the front door. The combination of heat and exhaustion had worn me out, and I sat for several minutes with the car door open and windows down, still wondering if we were doing the right thing, knowing that even if it wasn't, it was worth a try.

My alarm clock went off early as I had set it to the night before. I woke surprised by the fact that I'd fallen asleep at all and quickly readied myself to go to the hospital.

Only a few cars were on the road for the half-mile drive. I easily found my way back to the hospital and to the emergency entrance, the one I'd been instructed to use at that hour. As I passed through, I was reminded of Jon's many, many ER visits, and I felt a clamp tighten in the middle of my gut. In that moment I knew Jon was right to choose this treatment. He didn't deserve to live his life in emergency rooms and dangling on the edge of survival. This was worth a try.

I was directed by someone to the elevator and from there, I knew my way to find Jon. We almost ran into each other as I got off on the adolescent floor, and Jon, in a wheelchair being pushed by staff, was about to get on.

"Hi, Mom," he said as I joined him in the lift, and the nurse pushed the button to the treatment floor.

"Hey Jon. Did you sleep?"

"Not really. You ready?" he asked.

I nodded. My hands were sweaty and my chest burdensome, but I was here and ready to support his decision.

The nurse behind the wheelchair chimed in.

"Here we go, then," she said as she pushed the wheelchair forward off the elevator and turned left to meet Dr. Peters.

Ann Kremer is a registered nurse who works in an emergency room and understands the current epidemic of mental health issues in our country. As a first-time author, she shares her tumultuous journey of raising her son who experienced mental illness while living on a small island in the Puget Sound. She hopes those who struggle with mental illness, and those that love them, may find a slice of hope in her beautifully written memoir and to know they are not alone.

Birth Days

By Rebecca Mabanglo-Mayor

A NICU nurse bundled Tali into layers of a blanket, tucking the folds neatly across and over her tiny frame before the photographer took his shot. A white blanket with a blue stripe covered her white onesie, then a light pink blanket covered the first. In the photo, Tali rests on another blanket festooned with pictures of confetti, blue and pink ribbons, and yellow and blue balloons. Tali's hands folded over each other and under her chin, her head tilting slightly to one side as she stared serenely into the camera, lips pursed. Picture Day in the Neonatal Intensive Care Unit of Kapiolani Medical Center for Women and Children. When this picture was taken, I didn't know whether Tali would survive her first year. Weighing less than four pounds at birth because of her delivery eight weeks early, I feared her survival day to day, moment to moment.

In the picture, light reflects the fine sheen of soft blond hair that covered her body, a common phenomenon among premature babies. Term-birth babies typically shed this protective layer of hair in the final days before birth. Tali's head is covered with longer, dark hair, yet it's so sparse; she looks nearly bald. Perhaps the nurse smoothed her hair before the picture was taken. Brows barely visible, Tali looks slightly perturbed about having her picture taken yet also indulgent. I wonder if the flash bothered her eyes, if she wailed at the sensation like she did at any unexpected sound or sensation throughout her early childhood. I wouldn't put together that her terrible crying jags were due to her overwhelmed senses until much later, years in fact, too late for this small baby only eight days old.

I imagine they waited to take the picture until they knew Tali would survive. When she was first admitted into the NICU, they told my husband and me that she would have to stay there until her due date to be sure she thrived. She had to prove she could breathe, eat, eliminate, and hold her temperature fairly well despite her lack of body fat. Although it was normal for her to drop weight after birth, she'd have to prove that her body was absorbing nutrition. I imagine there was a battery of tests she was subjected to daily – blood tests, hearing and sight tests, awareness tests, muscle tests. Data gathering would be one way to think about all these little exams, but looking back, I wonder how this sense of being tested over and over might have affected her. Proving one's right to exist is a tiring thing for an adult let alone a baby who can barely turn her head.

Tali arrived eight days after my husband and I moved from Moscow, Idaho to Honolulu, Hawaii so he could attend graduate school at the University of Hawaii. We flew in after one last well-mother check that declared me fit for travel. Three days before Tali was born, my new OB-GYN said everything looked fine: cervix solid, no bleeding or fluid leaking. No reason to think premature birth was on the horizon. In fact, I turned out to be that stereotypical mother who didn't know she was in labor until I found myself in the ER with what I thought were gas cramps.

"You're nine cm dilated and I see hair," declared the ER nurse. "We're getting you to Labor and Delivery now." I didn't even have time to panic.

Fifteen minutes later, a nurse had Tali bundled and held her above me. Her hands rubbed her chin, and she looked for all the world like Jack Benny, the entertainer, and his expression: "Well, I'll be."

Well, I'll be.

My husband followed the nurses as they carried her to the NICU and I stayed behind, legs still propped in stirrups while a medical team stitched me up and made sure I wasn't going to bleed out because of the quick delivery. No spinal block, no anesthesia, just a local. The delivery was so quick that at one point, the doctor told me to stop pushing. Stop. What a silly thing for a male doctor to command. A woman's body just moves and births. There was no stopping. I wondered if I would die in that moment, like the beautiful, tragic mothers of so many movies I'd seen and books I'd read. A child is born under strange circumstances and suddenly, the medical team or mid-wife is scrambling. The camera pans up as the consciousness slips from the mother's eyes. Gone before anyone can prevent her leaving. I thought I would die.

Looking back, I realize, I wanted to die. Death was the only way to pay for whatever terrible mistake I had made that pushed this innocent child into the world too early.

"Your mother almost died when you were born," said my father one evening. Tali, a toddler by then. My husband and Tali were asleep in my old bedroom. I sat with my parents in the kitchen, a cup of tea cooling on the yellow Formica counter between us. My mother looked into her own mug of tea and shook her head.

"Oh, it wasn't that bad," she said. "Everything turned out fine."

My father pursed his lips and looked lost. Over thirty years had passed since the day I was born and I could see the moment haunted him. This was a story I hadn't heard yet.

"Died?" I asked.

"I thought I would lose you both," he replied. He tugged at his ear and took off his gold-rimmed glasses. "Your mother stopped breathing."

I looked at my mother who shook her head again and rocked back and forth like a child who'd been caught lying.

"I was fine," she insisted.

"Stopped breathing?" I said. I cast back to being in Kapiolani trying to remember if they put me on oxygen. There wasn't time, I guessed, and I never lost consciousness. I went up to the delivery room on a Code Purple, indicating a potentially life-threatening situation, and now I was learning that my own mother likely went Code Red, a definite life-threatening situation, while birthing me.

Neither of my parents spoke, yet I needed more.

"I remember you saying I was late," I prompted. "You were in labor three days..." I let my voice trail off in the hopes one of them would fill in the gaps.

"Yah, you were late," my mother replied. "Didn't want to come out. They were going to induce and I didn't want that. I pushed and pushed and pushed. You just didn't want to come."

She shrugged again as if to say that my father and I were making too much of such a small thing.

My father's hands shook as he picked up his cup and took a sip. He was still angry, still scared.

"She stopped breathing," he said. "They had to put a mask on her." He put his hand over his face as he struggled with a word.

I tried to imagine what it must have been like in that delivery room in the mid-60's. White sheets, a man behind a mask, covered head to toe in scrubs, murmuring instructions to a nurse beside my mother.

"Oxygen," I offered.

"Yes," he said. "Oxygen. They put a mask on her and I thought she would die."

"Too much anesthesia," my mother interjected matter of factly.

"Too much?" I replied, horrified that my own birth had been traumatic for her.

"I passed out," she replied. "They had to use forceps to get you out."

My hand involuntarily touched my head, the ghost of cold metal against my skin making my scalp tingle. I wondered why they didn't perform a C-section. Was it a problem with technology at the time or because she was a dark-skinned Filipina? Would a white woman have been left to labor so long? What was it like to be my mother in 1965 Seattle?

My mother folded and unfolded a white napkin between her finely manicured fingers, lost in the memory of the day I was born. Far from joy, I imagined she felt relief when I was finally born. I looked back to my father.

"She didn't die," I reassured, trying to smile. "And I didn't. We're here."

He wiped his eyes on a napkin and turned away.

In a pink photo album in the hallway closet was a small black and white picture of me as a baby with wild black hair and dark eyes, my hands raised up and covered with cloth. I suck my lower lip, my cheeks fat and full. I don't look like a baby who nearly died. I look small, not quite as small as Tali but still fragile in my blanket of white, my dark skin even darker against the white that surrounds me.

"If we were back in the Province," my mother told me later. "We would have probably died. It's a good thing we went to a hospital. Can you imagine me in a little hut having you?" She snorted at the thought. "See, back in the Philippines, you had to go to your mother's place when you had your baby. That's what your Lola did. I was born in Tulin where her mother lived."

I was surprised to hear this. My grandfather was a Philippine Scout stationed at Fort Stotsenburg before World War II. My grandmother, my Lola, lived in base housing with him and their two children at the time. I'd always figured my mom had been born on the base, but she hadn't.

My mother was six when the Japanese attacked the Philippines on the same day as the attack on Pearl Harbor. When Tali turned six, I tried to imagine her looking up at the sky like my mother did, watching all the planes fly overhead in perfect formation, her round face turned upward, brown eyes trying to take in the scope of the attack.

"I could hear the engines," my mother told me another day we sat in the kitchen together, the Formica counter between us littered with the pits of freshly eaten cherries. "Then there were the parachutes, big white ones. And there were bombs falling on the airstrip. They'd made decoy planes out of bamboo, and when they caught fire, they burned black smoke. We had to put handkerchiefs on our faces. We didn't know where my papa was. He'd gone to work in the morning and we ran up to Jack and Jill Hill close to my house when they attacked." She spread her hands wide as if to show the valley below the hill where they had run for cover. "We found these trees to hide near."

"What kind of trees, Mom?"

I thought about the mangroves and coconut trees I'd seen in Hawaii, wondering how much coverage they would give. She wouldn't have been alone with my Lola; they would have stood with my Lola's sister who was helping with the housework and my mother's younger sister who was four years old at the time.

"Trees," she replied with an apologetic shrug. Then I realized that as a six year old, she probably didn't know the names of trees, wouldn't have remembered such a small detail in the midst of the chaos.

I tried to wrap my mind around my mother as a six-year-old who, moments before, had been playing with her sister in their yard. My grandmother would have been 31, maybe 32, the same age I was when I gave birth to Tali. I started to calculate the distance between her siblings.

"Was Auntie Lily a baby at the time?"

"No," she replied, voice quiet. "Mama was pregnant. We were supposed to go up to the Province later so she could be born."

Pregnant and due any time given my aunt's birthday a month after the attack. Pregnant and protecting a six-year-old and a four-year-old. Pregnant and unsure if her husband was alive at all.

The bombs. The smoke. The terror. My Lola waited out the day, keeping her small family together until the attack ended sometime near sunset, and they made their way back to base housing. Miraculously, my grandfather appeared at their home, likely haggard and worried, covered in sweat and soot.

"Everyone was crying," said my mother. "I held on to my Papa. We didn't know if we would see each other again. My auntie packed food for us and we left for the Province by train the next morning. At the train station, there were so many people and then we heard the sirens again. WhooOOOooo! WhooOOOooo! We got off the train and hid under the cars. It's a good thing the engineer didn't try to leave or we'd have been crushed!"

Eventually the attack moved south to Manila, giving everyone a chance to board the train again and travel north. They arrived safely and found my grandmother's family. A month later, my aunt was born, and by the spring of '42, the combined US and Filipino military surrendered and the Japanese Occupation began. After the surrender, my grandfather was one of thousands who walked the Bataan Death March.

"We didn't know what happened to him after we left the base," said my mother. "Then one night I heard someone come into the house. I came into the kitchen and saw my Papa there.

He grabbed Mama around the waist. 'We lost,' he said. He was crying and then he fell over. He was so sick. Malaria."

My grandmother never shared memories of that time with me. How does a woman learn to mother during a war? How does she keep the uncertainty from crushing her? Maybe just keeping her daughters alive so they could be mothers was enough for her—to keep them fed on vegetables and rice and to tend her husband while he hid from Japanese patrols.

My mother doesn't know what time she was born. She's not even sure if the date on her birth certificate was accurate at all.

"We know it was winter," she said, "but the priest only came through once a week to say Mass. He baptized the babies and wrote down the days of when they were born. Sometimes he didn't come – maybe the rain made it too hard to travel – and so it might be awhile before a baby was baptized and the birth certificates were written. The old timers had a way of re-membering, but they are all gone now."

Tali's birthday and time are easy to remember. When they wheeled me up from the ER to Labor and Delivery, the intake nurse peppered me with questions even though my husband hovered nearby. First Name. Last Name. Date of birth. When I gave her my information she shook her head.

"That's today's date," she said, impatient with my struggle to speak through the pain. "What's *your* date of birth?"

A contraction gripped me and I screamed.

"Stop that!" she ordered. "You're fine. Date of birth?"

"Today *is* my birthday," I replied through my teeth, my pain so intense I didn't register her cruelty. Later I would work out the exact difference in age. Tali and I are 31 years, 364 days, 23 hours, and 16 minutes apart.

Her dark eyes narrowed as if she couldn't be sure if I was lying or delirious. My husband calmly confirmed my statement. Only then did she jot down the information. I felt someone move my legs into stirrups and she turned to my husband to complete the form.

Their voices mixed with the sound of the doctor directing nurses to do various tasks around me while I lay looking up at the examination light. Someone strapped a blood-pressure cuff to one arm. Someone else opened my vein so they could insert an IV line. I turned my head and saw a knot of people in scrubs hovering near a small sterile bassinette similarly lit, monitors ready.

My poor baby. Born on my birthday. Couldn't even give her a birthday of her own. Silently, I promised myself and her that she'd have the day all her own. I didn't need birthdays any more, not if remembering my birthday meant remembering this terror in my body, in my bones.

Then came the local anesthetic and the pushing. Finally the delivery was over. When they held her up for me to see, she had a surprised look on her face, startled to suddenly go from complete darkness to harsh light. I wanted to reach up and touch her, but maybe my hands were too dirty for that. Maybe I'd lost the right to hold her when my body rejected her presence.

I wanted to tell her I was sorry, that I took it all back, whatever went wrong. I just needed her to be ok.

Before I could speak, she was taken to the NICU where, later in the day, my nurse wheeled me to see her. Even though I had washed my hands up to my elbows like the nurse directed, I still didn't dare touch Tali. Instead, I plucked at the blanket she lay on and looked at the monitors. Wires snaked from sensors on her body to a grey box with a cord that fed data to a screen above my head. I tried to decipher the green lines and numbers: respiration, heart rate, oxygen levels. Nearby, other monitors were hooked to other babies and the NICU was noisy with the whirr and ping of machines doing what they needed to do to keep the babies alive.

Besides the monitor sensors and a diaper, Tali wore an oxygen line around her face. I asked the nurse if Tali would need intubation. My mother would want to know that detail, once I had the courage to call and tell her what had happened.

"No," the nurse replied, her voice cheerful and confident. "In fact, I think the doctor will order the oxygen removed. Baby is breathing okay on her own."

Relieved, my thoughts turned to the early morning cramps that had brought us to the hospital: why did she come so early?

Predictably, my mother had the same question when I called her later in the day.

"Did you fall?" she asked sounding very much like the irritated nurse who took my stats earlier in the day.

"No," I said. "I don't know what happened."

"What did the doctor say?"

"They're sending the placenta in for testing," I replied. "I don't know when we'll get the results." It felt like an excuse, a delaying tactic.

Did my Lola similarly question my mother when I was born? Did my Lola know my mother had nearly died from an overdose of anesthesia? Or did my mother choose not to tell her anything? After all, my Lola had birthed six daughters, a pair of twins rounding out the family around the time the war ended. Maybe my mother felt inadequate too.

"I can't come," said my mother, leaping to answer a question I had not asked. "We have plane tickets for October. She wasn't supposed to come until October."

Later I would realize she was still in shock from my news, perhaps fighting the tradition that she should be there for me, like her mother had been there for her, and so on when my Lola was a new mother.

In the moment, though, I was grateful she wouldn't be coming. As far as I knew, I'd had the first premature child in the family, and so there were things that would be different. I didn't know how. I didn't know what we were going to face the next day, the next week, the next year. I just knew I needed to try and learn it all on my own. Like my Lola faced a war that raged across her Province and my mother faced in a new country where she was persistently undervalued, I'd learn to face my own battles and become a mother too.

Rebecca Mabanglo-Mayor's non-fiction, poetry, and short fiction have appeared in print and online in several journals and anthologies including *Katipunan Literary Magazine, Growing Up Filipino II: More Stories for Young Adults, Kuwento: Small Things,* and *Beyond Lumpia, Pansit, and Seven Manangs Wild: An Anthology.* Her poetry chapbook *Pause Mid-Flight* was released in 2010 and her collection of poetry and essays, *Dancing Between Bamboo Poles* is forthcoming.

Obedience

By Cami Ostman

I stood when Basil Sparks lifted his hands to the sky and shouted, "Get on your feet for the Lord." The room was full of adolescent perspiration and pheromones. Two hundred of us stood, praising God, singing, "As the deer panteth for the water, so my soul longeth after thee, oh Lord." My best friend Grace, a tall girl whose tanned beauty eclipsed everyone who was ever seen with her, was on one side of me and Hedda, the bespectacled, white-haired, pale-skinned girl from church was on the other side.

The auditorium at this Christian campground was packed, front to back, side to side with us, aged twelve to eighteen, all with our hands in the air, singing to God. The lights lowered and the piano music quieted, as Basil hummed the tune from behind his thick black mustache. He was so beautiful that I had trouble keeping my eyes closed to worship. Beside me Grace reached for the sky and let tears stream unfettered down her face. I never cried during worship.

In fact, I rarely cried at all anymore, but I wished I could—I thought it would be a relief. The last time I cried was last year after my stepfather followed me around the kitchen criticizing the way I cleaned up after dinner. I'd ignored him, thinking that since I couldn't get him to stop bullying me, at least I could pretend he didn't exist. My obstinacy had made him mad and he'd hit me in the face. I don't know how I did it, but I kept cleaning, like it hadn't happened. So he'd hit me again. My mother watched from the living room couch in a stupor of depression, but my little brother ran into the kitchen and jumped on his back. And that's when I started to cry—for my brother to get away so he wouldn't get hurt. I cried that night in my room too. Hard. But not since then. And for sure never in public.

I just didn't feel God the way Grace did. Didn't feel His presence or see miracles all around me, though I did crave what Grace described: A God who lived inside of you, so you were never alone in your body. "Even if your own parents hate you," Grace told me once when I stayed at her house to seek refuge from one of my mother's dark episodes, "God never leaves your heart." I wanted to believe her. So much.

From the front, Basil indicated that the musicians should stop playing altogether, and there was a long, silent, and pregnant breath held as we all waited for the Word of Knowledge. The Word of Knowledge was Basil's specialty. He was particularly attuned to the Spirit. That's why we were all here. These quarterly retreats—"Sought Out" they were called—were weekend getaways where we came to hear God's direct messages to us. Basil, thirty-years-old, lean, olive-skinned with kind eyes and a sultry, smoky voice, led us in worship and prayer, gave us a sermon about purity and devotion, and then listened to the Lord on our behalf. In a moment, he would begin calling people out by name or, if he didn't know your name, he would just point at you. You would pay close attention and he would tell you what God was saying to you.

We all stood, immobile, both hoping and dreading that God was going to notice us. But I prayed for Basil to see me, to point at me and to say, "Young lady, the Lord has a Word for you." I craved to be known by God. To be spoken to instead of shouted at. I yearned for it the way you yearn for summer when school finally lets out in June. I needed to know God cared about my life. That's why I followed Grace to the first row. Because I would never put myself front and center the way Grace would. I lacked my best friend's entitlement and showmanship, but I knew the front row was the best place for God to see you.

Grace and I had been best friends for three years by now. Since the eighth grade we'd been inseparable. At first we were a part of a trio with Suzye, but Suzye had left us. Last year when we were freshmen she'd become pregnant by her boyfriend, who was 21, and had gotten married. I was her maid of honor, walking down the aisle of our church in a dress I'd borrowed from the piano player. Suzye had a little baby now and when I did talk to her, she said things like, "I never sleep. Just wait until you have babies!" I'd already promised myself I would never have children, but I didn't bother telling this to Suzye. She seemed to take comfort from the idea that one day, I would be as sleep deprived as she was.

Basil moaned from the stage. This meant God was talking to him. I sucked in more breath. When he opened his eyes, they shined out at us. He scanned the auditorium. "Jenny, where are you?" he finally said. "Jenny Sanchez? I know you're here but I can't see you. The Lord has a Word for you. Everyone, can you have a seat. Jenny, stay standing."

We all sat with one collective movement. Jenny, as it turned out, was in the row behind us. I didn't know her. The room was full of kids from more than two-dozen churches. I only knew the kids from Good Life Center, the church Grace and her family attended, where Basil was the youth pastor and where Grace went to youth group on Wednesday nights. Sometimes my mother let me go along with her even though she seriously disapproved of my going to church. Fact was, to come to this weekend retreat I'd lied to my mother and told her I was camping with Grace's family. She hadn't wanted to let me go but relented in the end. I felt bad about that lie as I sat in the pew now, but I tried to put my guilt out of my mind to listen to Basil give his Word.

I turned around to look at Jenny, a short girl with brown skin and thick glasses. She held onto the chair in front of her. "Jenny, dear, how are you?"

Jenny blinked back tears. She looked scared if you asked me. "I'm okay," she said.

"But I wonder," Basil paused and studied her from his perch on the elevated stage, "have you been worrying? About one of your parents? About your dad?"

Jenny nodded. Tears practically sprayed out of her eyes, but she didn't make a sound. The girl next to her reached over and took Jenny's hand. "He's got cancer."

"Yes, that's what the Lord is telling me. It's in his midsection, is that right?"

"Stomach." Now Jenny let out a sob.

My own throat closed up at this point. This was the second Sought Out retreat I'd snuck away from my family to get to, and I'd never heard so much detail in one of Basil's Words. Usually they were like, "God says he loves you." Or "God wants you to forgive someone." The kind of things you could find in the little horoscope scrolls in the grocery store checkout line. How did Basil know all of this about Jenny's dad? I whipped my head around to look at Grace. Was she as amazed by this as I was? But she looked perfectly calm. In fact, her eyes were closed and she had her hand outstretched toward Jenny in a gesture of prayerful support, silently whispering, "Thank you Jesus," under her breath. Later I would ask her if Basil knew Jenny's family, but I shouldn't interrupt her praying now.

"The Lord wants you to know that the best thing you can do for your dad is to be a comfort to him, Jenny."

Jenny nodded.

"God has this in His hands. You're not to question this. Not to doubt the Lord because of this. God wants you to know that He loves you and loves your dad, and you are not to lose faith."

Jenny nodded again.

"Okay, sweetheart? You just keep your eyes on Him."

Jenny sat down and began to sob. The kids around her put their hands on her and started to speak in tongues—long multi-syllabic repetitive sentences punctuated with vowel sounds that took a downward tonal turn. Quietly, though, so they didn't disrupt Basil's channel to God.

My throat was burning now. With envy. Why didn't God have a message like this for me? I turned back to face the stage, to watch Basil revert back into his trance of deep listening. The moments ticked by as we all waited to hear who God would talk to next. Wait. Wait. Me. Me. Me. Please.

And then. His eyes popped open and he was looking right at me.

"Cami."

I didn't even know Basil knew my name. I'd only been a few times to his Wednesday night services. I looked up at him. My heart pounded. Grace thrust her supportive hand in my direction and squeezed her eyes shut tighter, praying hard.

"You've got some troubles at home, don't you?"

That was for sure. I was quiet.

"Can you stand up, dear?"

I stood.

My knees quivered. The whole room—these two hundred kids—were looking at me. I stopped breathing.

"The Lord wants you to know that He sees what is happening. He knows everything. Every last thing that's going on. Do you understand?"

Now I got scared. Basil knew I'd lied to be able to come here, didn't he? How did I think God wouldn't be mad at me for that lie and wouldn't tell Basil to chastise me? Did I think just because I was coming to worship God He would let me get away with a lie? What was everyone going to think of me? Would any one in this room talk to me after tonight? I hadn't even told Grace that I'd used her family in my falsehood. Would she tell her dad to call my mom? And what would happen to me when I got home? Fear turned my face red and now tears did spring to my eyes, though I refused to let them flow.

But then Basil shook his head and looked at me with compassion, "Sweetheart, He sees your pain." I let my breath out and felt my heart slow down. "And He is telling me to tell you something important."

I nodded, waiting for more, still hoping God would not accuse me in front of everyone. A flash of terrible guilt trickled down my body from head to toe like someone had cracked a giant raw egg over my head. Here God was being nice to me and I'd lied to my mom. But then I thought about how last week my mother had grabbed me by the hair and yanked me hard when I showed exasperation at having to cook dinner while she "talked through issues" with her husband holed up in their bedroom. And I thought of how my stepfather came out of their room when we got loud in the living room and shouted and poked my little brother's chest until he'd backed him against the wall. My brother's tiny torso caved in to protect his chest bone from the thump, thump of our stepdad's pounding.

We all stayed quiet while Basil listened for what more God wanted to tell me. Basil sighed. "Help is on the way," he said, now burning me up with his perfect, gorgeous brown eyes.

I felt my heart open. "Oh," I said aloud while Grace whispered thank you to Jesus beside me.

And then, "Only one more thing Cami, and then I sense the Lord wants us to close our service for the night and all go to bed—prayerfully." The piano player fingered the keyboard gently. The soft background music calmed me as I waited for the final Word. "God tells me He wants you to know that your obedience is your witness. Your goodness is your testimony. Do you understand that?"

I nodded, of course, though I wasn't completely sure what he meant. Part of me deflated. Obedience was hard when the rules were different day to day. But I would try.

Basil winked at me. And with that, he cued the musicians and started singing softly, "Oh Lord, You're beautiful. Your face is all I seek. And when Your eyes are on this child, Your grace abounds to me. Everyone join me now!" I sat down as the rest of the auditorium stood up for the song.

This wasn't what I'd hoped for when I was praying that God would speak to me. I guess I'd hoped for something magic. Something like, "God is telling me there is a long-lost aunt who wants to take you in and move you across the country." Instead, I'd been told to be good.

Grace, Hedda, and I went back to our cabin. The smell of cedar wood and campfire followed us inside as we gathered on Grace's bed, each of us appropriately solemn after Basil's Word. Our cabin counselor was in the shower and the other three girls, all from a different church, who occupied the remaining beds, were giggling and talking about the boys in the cabin next to ours. One of them had a boyfriend over there.

Grace gazed at me meaningfully and rubbed my back a little as we got settled. "Let's hold hands and pray that the help Basil said was on the way for Cami will come fast!" she said. She knew my mom was sad. And mean. And loud. And that my stepfather scared me.

Grace grabbed our hands; Hedda and I submitted and held hands with each other too. But I couldn't pray until I confessed.

"I have to tell you both something," I said, looking first to Hedda, whose sweet albino face always appeared kind and accepting behind her thick glasses. Then I turned to Grace. Her hazel eyes were penetrating, like she could see my brain and my guts and not just my face.

"Spit it out, sister Cami," Grace said. She called me that sometimes, even at school, and I thought it was nice, like we were really a family and not just both God's children, like everyone was.

"Okay," I said. "Promise you won't judge me." They both nodded, so I plucked up some courage to outweigh my shame and said, "I lied to my mom to be able to come here."

Nobody moved. We sat there holding hands while Hedda's gaze went down to the space between us and Grace considered what was to be done. I could tell she was doing this because she had her eyes closed now like she was asking God for wisdom.

"Lying is against the Ten Commandments," Hedda finally said. "I think you have to pray and ask forgiveness."

I nodded. This sounded right.

Then Grace's eyes flew open. "And you have to tell your mom."

I shook my head. My armpits started sweating and I could feel my hands beginning to shake even though my friends held them tightly. Was that the right thing to do? Really? I knew telling the truth would cause big trouble. It wouldn't be safe. My mom could put me on restriction and I would have to pull out of the school play. She would tell my stepfather and then what? If I pulled out of the play, I would be home alone with him every day after school. I could think of ten different scenarios and none of them turned out with me being better off—or even unharmed—at the end. Grace might tell me that if I told the truth, God would protect me, but in my experience God was hit or miss in that department.

"Yep, you have to." Grace was firm. "Basil said that your obedience was your witness. 'Confess your sins one to another' the Bible says. That's that. If you don't do it, God won't send the help he promised. You have to, Cami. Do you agree, Hedda?"

Hedda continued to avoid looking at either of us. I was waiting for her to break the tie in my favor and to let me off the hook for telling my mother about my iniquity. When she looked up all she said was, "I don't know. I've never lied to my mom. But I think God will forgive you."

This wasn't sufficient for Grace. "God will forgive her, but until she is right in His eyes, He won't send help."

Hedda studied the pillow on the bed behind Grace. I could tell she wasn't sure what to do. "Sure," she said.

And my heart fell. So they both thought I should confess. Defeat and sorrow made me feel heavy.

Holding two soft, warm, feminine hands I told my next lie. "Okay," I said. "I'll tell her."

We bowed our heads and prayed for God to bring help to me quickly. Then we changed into our pajamas and I climbed into my bed, pretty sure that even though Basil had spoken to me, God still didn't see me.

Cami Ostman is the author of the memoir *Second Wind: One Woman's Midlife Quest to Run Seven Marathons on Seven Continents* and the editor of several anthologies. She's one of the founders of Red Wheelbarrow Writers in Bellingham, Washington and the CEO of *The Narrative Project* which supports writers in getting their books done.

Remembering You

Victoria (Tori) Peters

The first weekend in November didn't provide a clear sun-filled blue sky that opened to views of snow sparkling Cascade Mountains appearing so close I could almost touch them and reminding me why I loved the Pacific Northwest. No, instead clouds hung pregnant in the sky, waiting for their time. The gray of dawn continued into the daytime hours and into the early evening too. It was exactly the right kind of day for sitting around waiting for something to happen.

Sarah, a third grader and my youngest of four children, had a swim meet that Saturday. Matt, Nick, and Maria, all teenagers, chose to spend the day at home. I trusted them; our seven years living in Africa had instilled the ability to keep themselves busy. They had their chores, homework, and hobbies. Matt played the guitar and could spend hours writing music and playing songs. Nick read. I could not keep up with his voracious appetite for books. Maria created earrings and necklaces from beads she bought with her babysitting money and then sold to family and friends.

And there was always television. The kids had been deprived of popular U.S. shows and music for the seven years we'd lived in Mali, Rwanda, and Tunisia. The most negative aspect of growing up without television and radio from their perspective was their lack of knowledge of pop culture, and now they were making up for lost time. I figured the three would spend most of this day in front of the television. And I was fine with it.

We'd been back in the U.S. for only 18 months since leaving our last post, Tunis, Tunisia. My husband Ron, a diplomat in the State Department, was presently assigned to the administrative position at the embassy in Kabul, Afghanistan. Two years earlier, he'd written on the bottom of his transfer list of 15 possible posts, "I will consider the admin position in Kabul."

"Delete it," I'd said.

"Think about it," he responded. "The kids and you can go back to the States to spend time with our families, and Matt and Maria need braces anyway." He had his mind made up and would not listen to my arguments.

Several months later, the phone rang. The kids and I'd been home all week confined to the house because of school closure, but the embassy had not closed. I picked up the ringing phone and his voice on the other end said, "It came through. Kabul. I've been assigned to Kabul."

"Turn it down," I said.

"What?"

"Turn down the offer."

"We'll talk about it when I get home."

That evening and the next couple of days strong words went between us. But in the end I couldn't convince him to turn down the assignment and resigned myself to the fact that I'd be a single parent with three teenagers and an elementary age child.

The civil war in Afghanistan had begun five years earlier in 1978. In 1979, the Russians entered the war to support the communist government ruling out of the capital, Kabul. The U.S. government was making plans to close the embassy and Ron's job was to dispose of the inventory from the hospital, school, U.S. AID, and all matter of material things needed to house and support a once large U.S. mission.

What kept us sane during our separation was knowing that every three or four months he would be home for a month. When he left August 1982, I knew he'd be home for Christmas, in March, and for a month in the summer. But his letters home sometimes mentioned things like how he slept under the grand piano in his living room on nights when the bombs from the *mujahideen*, the Afghan resistance fighters, lit up the night sky.

I kept my worries to myself and the kids never asked what Ron wrote in his letters to me. Besides I knew my worrying would not keep Ron safe, so I kept myself busy with the children and their activities, making friends, and spending much needed time with family.

When Sarah and I returned from the swim meet, JoJo, our dog, met us at the door with his tail wagging back and forth. I could hear snippets of music and words from MTV, "...Just can't you see /We've got everything, do you even know we know? / every time you go away /You take..."

Umm, I thought, Paul Young. The first time I'd heard that song I felt it had been written for Ron and me. Young's song was one of the few pop songs I did not have to ask the kids who was singing. I'd think of the line "You take a part of me," and wonder how many parts Ron took every time he left. Especially when his letters proclaimed how much he needed me.

"Yoo-hoo, we're home," I said to the three heads turned to the screen, eyes glued on the dancing. Matt, Nick and Maria turned away from the television briefly to greet Sarah and me.

"How was your day?" I asked and wondered if they'd ever moved away from the couch and if the kitchen had been cleaned.

"Oh, hey Mom, there were several phone calls during the day," Matt said.

"And?" I said, waiting for more information. A new music video began.

"I think it was the State Department."

His answer took me by surprise. "Did they tell you why they were calling? Did they leave a number?" I asked. The State Department didn't just call to chat; they would be calling to tell me something about Ron. And they didn't typically call to give good news. I was glad Matt wasn't alarmed, but I felt an inkling of fear creep into me.

"No, they just wanted to talk to you," he said, turning back to the MTV Channel.

I could have asked whether it was a man or a woman? What did the voice sound like? Was it calm or anxious? But Matt didn't know anything else, so why badger him for information he didn't have? I left the kids in the rec room and went directly upstairs to the kitchen to make a cup of coffee, which I suddenly needed. The kids had done dishes and cleaned up their lunch makings; I smiled to myself. A bright spot in the day.

With my hands warming as I held the hot coffee mug, I went into the living room to sit in the oak rocker and wait for the phone to ring. Ron had found the rocker at a secondhand store before we were married. Our first year together while I was pregnant with Matt, we both worked on sanding and rubbing the linseed oil into the wood. We'd covered the seat in a dark brown. Our four children had been nursed and rocked to sleep in it.

As I rocked and sipped, I wondered if the State Department would call back today. The three-hour time difference made it almost 7:00 P.M in D.C. How long would I have to wait? Should I do something? I could start dinner, but I wasn't hungry yet. The open curtains revealed a gray day turning into a wet, windy evening. The patter of the rain hitting the windows cut into my longing for Ron that was never far below my surface.

The phone rang. I jumped and rushed into the kitchen to take the receiver off the wall.

"Hello," I said, trying to breathe deeply to calm my pounding heart.

A man's voice, "Mrs. Peters?"

"Yes," I replied.

He identified himself as a Foreign Service Officer on the Bureau Desk. *Get on with it. What's wrong?* I wanted to say, but I waited patiently.

"I'd like to reassure you this is not an emergency." His words relieved some of the tightness I felt in my throat. *Why call me several times on a Saturday for a non-emergency?*

"I'm calling because there's been an incident at the embassy in Kabul which will probably be in the news tomorrow morning. We'd like you to know before we give the go-ahead to the press to release the story."

What could be bad enough to make the news but not cause me to panic? The white coiled phone cord stretched as I walked around through the door leading into the dining room and leaned against the wall. The light from the kitchen and living room slid around my grandmother's round oak table and old chairs. The two blown-up photos of the lioness Ron had taken on our final trip to the Akagera Game Park in Rwanda stared at me from the opposite wall. A moment in time when we caught the only lion we had seen in the six trips we had made over a period of two years when we lived in Kigali. We'd had a life of adventure; that was for sure.

The voice went on, "The Afghan army has surrounded the embassy..."

I tried to pay close attention, but the voice in my head whispered over his, *This is what one of those calls feels like.* I slid down the wall and sat on the floor with my back to the wall.

"Okay," I said. *Ron will be alright. Ron will be all right. We've been in tight situations before and survived. He'll be okay.*

"Apparently, a Russian soldier has entered the American Embassy Compound and asked for asylum. The Afghan army has surrounded the embassy and cut electrical power to the embassy. No one can leave. But everyone is okay." *For now,* I thought.

"Thank you." I said, hung up the phone, and returned to the rocker. How do I respond to this? What am I supposed to do? How frightened for Ron do I need to be? Temporarily paralyzed, love and a fierce sense of longing ran through me. I did not want to face life without him. The fellow from the State Department—I had already forgotten his name—had assured me that this was not an emergency and everyone was all right. I decided I needed to let logic rule over feelings somehow. What needed to be done now?

I descended the stairs to the TV room. I couldn't let the children know I was afraid for Ron, even though I was—very afraid. I thought of word pictures in his letters of the tanks "spewing death" and his angry words describing the Russian car filled with young men, not much older than our sons, killed when their car blew up on the street just down from the embassy.

I had not named the feeling I had when I'd read his letters. I didn't allow their negative energy to interfere with my task of raising four children. To dwell on my sadness and aloneness, the terrible ache of not having the person I wanted to share life with, was not in my nature. As I stepped on the bottom stair, I clung to the positive words I'd heard on the phone, "This is not an emergency."

I stood in front of the kids and said, "Turn the television off. We've got to talk."

The kids looked at me and knew by my tone not to argue. Nick turned the TV off.

"I just talked to a man from the State Department on the Kabul desk." All four kids looked at me, waiting. I continued, "A Russian soldier came into the American Embassy Compound asking for asylum and now the Afghan army has surrounded the premises. Dad is okay, but he can't leave and he can't call. This will probably be on the news tomorrow."

Matt responded with the words I'd been thinking, "Dad will be all right. He knows how to get out of tight situations." I nodded in agreement. Sarah crawled up onto my lap.

We talked about what it meant when a soldier asked for asylum. I knew no details, so we could only speculate on why the young man was asking for help from the United States.

As we talked, I realized how our years in Africa and our experience living through a violent strike there had prepared us to pull together as a family unit. We sat in silence hanging on to the thought that Matt had expressed. Ron would get out of this. In our minds he had no choice.

Fortunately Maria shook us all out of our paralysis by asking, "What are we having for dinner?" Leave it to a child to stay in the moment.

Ah, yes, something I can do.

I didn't feel like cooking. Our discussion about where to go for dinner took our minds off of Ron's situation. We settled on a restaurant and I said, "Don't forget your jackets. It is pouring out."

Nick sped out of the house before anyone else could even put their shoes on. His goal was always to sit shotgun since both he and Matt had grown taller in the eighteen months we'd been home and their legs no longer fit comfortably in our small white Toyota station wagon. I heard the door slam shut as he left the house.

I stood in the hallway threading my arms into my jacket, when I heard the front door open again and Nick came running back in calling, "Mom, Mom, look what I just found."

I looked up from zipping my coat to see a very wet, black creature nestled in his arms.

"Mom, isn't it cute!"

It was a ferret. Nick had wanted one for a long time and had gone through a stage when he was constantly showing me pictures of ferrets and asking for one as a pet. Ron and I had both said no.

I immediately felt tired. This was ridiculous. What force had brought this water-soaked animal into my life now? And on the same day my husband was holed up in the U.S. Embassy surrounded by the Afghan army?

"Mom, can you believe it's a ferret. I saw something running under the car. I caught it. Can I keep it?"

Was the universe playing with me? I ignored his question.

Obviously this was not a wild animal. The wet critter had snuggled into Nick's jacketed arms. JoJo jumped up and down on Nick's legs trying to reach the ferret. Now Sarah and Maria came running into the hall. Chaos seemed to whirl around me. I couldn't think.

"Isn't it cute!" Nick stated this more than asked as the girls tried to see the creature.

Matt ran up the stairs to see what all the commotion was about. "A wet ferret," he exclaimed. "Where did that come from?"

"I saw it running under the car and caught it. Isn't it cute?"

I felt my head would explode. At the back of my mind was the memory that my husband was in danger, but in front of me the rest of the family was hyperfocused on this wet creature.

"JoJo, sit." I said at the dog.

I couldn't turn the animal loose in this weather, that much was clear. My children would see that as cruel. But I really didn't want it in the house. Their pleading eyes looked at me for a decision. Looking directly in Nick's face, I sighed and said, "Take a box from the garage and put it in your room for now. Make sure the door is closed tightly. We'll talk about what to do with it at dinner."

A run-away ferret and Russian soldier both seeking asylum the same night. At least no one had surrounded our house. Our electricity was still on. But I had to get away and catch my breath.

Between bites of pastrami sandwiches, french fries, hamburgers, and salad (for me), we talked about the ferret. We discussed ways Nick could let people know he'd found a missing 'run-away ferret.' He agreed to ask kids on the school bus and in his classes. He said he would put notices up around the neighborhood. I thought the weather would not be conducive to paper notices on telephone poles, but didn't discourage him. Matt, Maria, and Sarah would ask their friends, too, if any had heard of someone missing a pet ferret.

Back at home, I helped Nick make an area in his room for the ferret. It was not to leave his room, I made it very clear. Priscilla, the cat, sniffed around the outside of Nick's door. JoJo sat waiting to be let into the room. They were curious, and I could see they wouldn't settle down. All I wanted was a little peace. "Maybe we should let them check each other out," I suggested, thinking we should get the meeting over with. Nick held the ferret as we tried to introduce the three. Priscilla's hairs stood up on her tail and she spat at the animal. JoJo barked. Neither seemed happy that there was a new resident in the house. I understood the feeling.

That night I watched the news. President Reagan was getting ready for a summit meeting with Gorbachev. The Russian soldier and the embassy were not mentioned. I thought about Nick and my little war when he'd decided he wanted a pet ferret months earlier. He could be as stubborn as Ron when it came to something he wanted. Nick's campaign for a pet ferret had gone on for weeks. Finally, I wooed him away from the ferret with an enticement of going to summer camp. It worked. I felt his choice to go to a horseback riding camp in the Cascades was an excellent compromise and the Ferret War ended. So why did this ferret appear now in our lives?

Ron's brother and my father called on both Sunday and Monday to see if I had heard any more news. I hadn't, but I wasn't completely out of my mind with fear. No news might actually be good news. I figured if tragedy struck, I would be hearing *something* from the State Department. Yet because the department had called me repeatedly on Saturday, I found it upsetting that there was now only silence. Was it really happening? As I waited for some word, I got to wondering: who was this asylum seeker who was causing me so much concern and worry?

Meanwhile the ferret was happening for sure. Sunday Nick called his friends in the neighborhood. No luck in finding the owner. We were still stuck with this little furry intruder.

Monday after school, Nick dropped his school bag in his room and came up to the kitchen. "Do you know where the ferret is?" he asked, opening the refrigerator door.

I stopped in the middle of washing a dish and looked at him, confused. "In your room." *At least he'd better be.*

"No, it isn't. The door was open a little bit."

I could feel my blood start to boil. I was barely holding myself together without news about the situation in Afghanistan. But I didn't want to explode on my child. Knowing Nick's room was a disaster, I tried to sound calm. "Did you look for it?"

"Yes."

I dried my hands on my jeans, took a breath, and the search for the ferret was on. Where does one begin to look for a ferret? Behind the washer, dryer, television set, bookcases, under beds, chairs, desks, and tables. We found no ferret. JoJo thought he would help and followed me into the kitchen as I debated about moving the refrigerator. Then he followed me into the living room where Priscilla sat on the window sill behind the sofa looking down at the floor rather than out the window, as she would normally do. I called to the boys. When they came up, I asked them to help me turn over the sofa. As we did, that ferret came scurrying out. Nick grabbed him and took him downstairs again.

I stood and assessed the damage. The ferret had ripped apart the lining under the sofa and hidden inside. There was a mess to clean up. That was it. I was at the end of patience and had to get control of something. My ultimatum: the ferret had to leave by Friday. No argument accepted.

The next couple of days were a blur of driving kids to swim team practices, volunteering at school and church, waiting and waiting for news of Ron. I moved through activities numbly, as if reality were holding me hostage every bit as much as the Afghan army was holding Ron and his colleagues hostage.

Finally, on Friday, Nick found a home for the ferret. And I received a call saying the Russian soldier had left the embassy with the Russian Ambassador. What diplomatic posturing and words had flown back and forth between the American and Russian Ambassadors? What would happen to that poor kid, sent away with the Russians instead of getting the protection he'd hoped for?

But I could breathe. Ron was alright. Everyone at the embassy was alright.

All was well. The ferret was gone. Our lives went on. November winds and rains replaced the troubles of the ferret and the soldier. Thanksgiving was celebrated. Advent brought the preparations for Christmas and, finally, Ron returned the middle of December.

At the airport, I waited at Customs anxiously as people began coming through the doors. His tired eyes brightened and a smile broke through his full beard when he saw me. I placed my arms around his broad chest and his strong arms encircled me. We held each other for a long minute before walking down to the baggage claim.

On the ride home, I told him about the ferret fiasco. Ron laughed and said he was glad he hadn't had to deal with a displaced ferret—as if he'd rather deal with the Afghan army! I could finally laugh too.

At home, while he unpacked, I sat on the bed. He took a small silk envelope out of his bag and placed it in my hand. I opened it and found a gold colored button. I felt its lightness and roundness and ran my fingers over the raised five legged star with a hammer and sickle stamped in the center. Then I looked at Ron to explain.

"He was just a kid," he said to me. "He wanted to go home. He spoke some German, so I spoke to him. The war didn't make sense to him and he just wanted to go home. But we couldn't help him. He would have been stuck at the embassy for the rest of this unending war. Tori, he was just a kid," Ron shook his head sadly. "He was two years older than Matt. When he left, he gave me the button and said, 'Remember me.'"

"But what happened to him? Wasn't he a deserter from the Soviet Army?" I said. The word brought up a picture in my head of a firing squad.

Ron looked at me and said, "The agreement was that he would be sent somewhere else. Who knows what will happen to him."

We looked at each other with an understanding that he would probably never find his way back to his home and family.

I stood up and held Ron tight. I would always pair the memory of the ferret fiasco with my fears of losing Ron and now my sense of sorrow over the plight of this unknown Russian soldier. This pairing would ease the memory of that stretch of time for me. But Ron would always carry the burden of the reality of this young man's fears and unmet desire for freedom.

Victoria (Tori) Peters writes, travels, reads, and is grandmother of four grandchildren. Since she retired from teaching, she walked the Camino de Santiago across the Pyrenees Mountains to Santiago, Spain and on to the Atlantic Ocean, climbed to the Tiger's Nest in Bhutan, trekked the Andes Mountains to Choquequirao, Peru, and visits Taipei, Taiwan every year.

Uncovering the Warrior Within

By Kristi Lyn Reddy

Another sharp blow to my side forced me to curl up tighter. He walked past me, and I kept my hands covering my head unsure of what would come next. My beating heart battled for attention against the intense throbbing in my head. I couldn't feel him near me anymore. Where did he go? The second hand ticking on the wall clock slowed my rapid heartbeat as I focused on the rhythmic beat. No other sound but our breathing. He was still in the room.

I moved my hands from my head to the floor. Palms pressed into the carpet as I forced my upper body to move, my right eye cried out in pain as my eyelashes stirred. I noticed a ringing in my right ear and felt something warm tickle my earlobe. I reached my hand up to touch it and brought it back down under me as I continued to face the ground then opened my left eye, keeping my right eye closed for the moment. My breath pulled in, dark red blood on my finger, a wave of nausea rolled through my gut. Pushing past the pain, I dared to open my right eye. A sea of blurriness sent tremors through my entire body.

"I can't see out of my eye." Panic in my voice met with silence. "My right eye, it's not working." My breathing erratic, panting, gasping for air.

A short blast of sadistic laughter filled the room. I waited for him to speak.

"I was going to kill you. You have no idea just how lucky you are. That damn bowl. I was going to pick that glass bowl up and smash it over your head. Had it in my grasp, but the fucking thing stuck to the table."

The laughter again.
"*It* would have killed you."
My blood was ice.

That evening I was glad our daughter Laurie was at Kaylee's house. Kaylee was a home school friend, both girls 10 years old and in the fourth grade. Don refused to allow his daughter to go to public school. He held a firm belief that public school would lead his little girl down a road to wrong friends, drugs, alcohol and getting pregnant.

I locked myself in the bathroom and cleaned my wounds in the bath, lingering as long as I dared. Glancing at Laurie's empty bedroom as I headed to my room, everything within me longed to crawl into her bed, alone. I knew better. Although he might leave me be for the night, there was no telling the consequence I would face if I tried to hide. No, it was best to go to him now, go to sleep if I was lucky, tell him sorry if he would listen, seek forgiveness for what I had done to anger him. I slipped into bed careful not to disturb him. His breathing shallow, either asleep or feigning sleep. The sheet pulled tight up to my chin, I lay in the silence, my mind empty of thought. To say I slept would be a lie. In the morning, Don was calm. Like he'd been satiated. He even asked me how I'd slept while I scurried around the kitchen making him coffee. By the time I left for work, I almost wondered if last night had happened.

Throughout that day and in the days to come I wondered again, for the millionth time, how to keep Don happy. Last night's fight had ensued after I'd glanced at the clock while he was lecturing me. I'd tried to do it discreetly, but he'd caught me. Some part of me had known he would see my glance as disrespect, but I'd been so tired, so incredibly tired. And to be honest, I knew it had been disrespectful. God charged me with respecting my husband and I couldn't figure out how to do it. It isn't that I didn't want to, it was just that Don made it hard. I struggled to be the submissive wife, the Proverbs 31 woman, God called me to be. I didn't yet know the warped sense of submission I was living under. Between the sermons at the pulpit multiple times a week and my own daily bible study, my mind was full of God's word. Inevitably Don's voice of criticism rang the loudest when I got it wrong time and again. My desire to be a 'woman whose children called her blessed' and 'whose husband praised her' pushing me to stay and try harder. In daily prayers, I begged God to help me get it right and for my husband to love me like Christ loved the church.

Two months later, on a December evening, I walked into our split-level townhome, our ten-year-old daughter, Laurie, right behind me, so close I could feel her breath. Neither of us spoke. My jaw hurt from constant clenching. I closed the door behind us, and we listened. Silence. No signs of life up the stairs or in the rec room as I flipped on the switch for the kitchen lights. It was early December and dark out already. We kept our voices at a hush.

"Sweetie, why don't you go to your room and unpack your things? I'll call you when dinner is ready, okay?" She'd stayed the previous two nights with Kaylee again, and Don and I had had an argument—not a fight, just some tension. At least I hoped that's all it would turn out to be.

"Sure, Mom." Laurie slipped through the living room, her feet noiseless on the carpet, and closed her bedroom door behind her. I marveled at how she knew when not to be heard and how often not be seen.

I put my coat and purse away and paused in the kitchen to check on items for dinner. Ground meat, tomato, cheese and tortillas. Tacos it is. A family favorite and quick to fix. My plan was to have a tree up and decorated before bedtime. That ought to smooth over the two-day-old rift still hovering between Don and me. I ignored the inner voice calling me a fool for thinking I could fill the house with good cheer with a Christmas tree.

Things between us were precarious. Between Don's quick temper and my childhood, which taught me to do as I was told, the marriage had been hard to hold together. I was doing my best, but I was clearly getting worse in terms of knowing how to soothe him, how to keep or make peace once I'd offended him. Tonight I hoped holiday spirit would help. But I was no dummy.

The acid in my stomach crept into my throat as I walked down the short hall to the bedroom I shared with my husband. The door was open just a crack. My fingers rested on the door frame and I took in a breath of courage before opening the door. He was sitting at the desk, his back to me. I ignored what he was feasting his eyes on at the computer monitor and instead focused my gaze on the carpet. Spit lake. Our daughter thought twice before walking around barefoot, repulsed by the sticky residue he deposited there daily. Saliva? Semen? I didn't ask.

"Hey, I'm home. How was your day?"

My question met with silence. Silence was never good.

"You know I was thinking, why don't you and Laurie go get a Christmas tree? I'll get dinner started. By the time you get back I'll have the food ready and we can eat while we decorate."

His back to me, he remained unmoved. I wrapped my arms around my stomach holding tight as if this might reduce the churning.

"Or... if you want to eat first I can hurry and cook dinner. It's just tacos, then we can all go grab the tree together. I just thought it might save time if you two went while I cook. What do ya think?" I realized I had twisted the sleeve of my sweater so tight the yarn had begun to unravel.

He rotated his body to face me. His arms crossed in front of him, resting on his pudgy belly. His weight had gone up and down over the years, often determined by whether or not he had a job. Right now he didn't.

I tried to read his face, to gauge the response forthcoming. His foot tapped the base of the chair as a stone-cold stare locked onto my face. I braced myself.

"Don't tell me what to do," he snarled.

My heartbeat raced. I couldn't get it right. After two entire days of silence and a full day to himself with me gone to work, I had hoped his wave of anger would be gone, leaving room for reconciliation. Obviously, this wasn't the case. I couldn't figure out how to keep from angering him. If I said nothing, I might be reprimanded for not planning for the night. And yet, if I spoke up and made suggestions I could be yelled at—or punished—for telling him what to do. He was the head of the family and I was to be a submissive obedient wife. Ephesians 5:22-23. He quoted it to me so often that I could say it from memory as well, 'Wives submit yourselves unto your own husbands, as unto the Lord. For the husband is the head of the wife...' The verse went on, but Don usually stopped right there when he lectured me. He never quoted the part about how husbands were supposed to love their wives.

I was a believer too. God honored marriage and, as Christ was the head of the Church, so was the husband head of the wife. That's what the Bible said. I wanted to please God and do right by my faith, but I was tired. So tired. And I didn't have any idea that maybe, possibly, there was some notion in God's mind that I was more important than this marriage. I had no idea that my well-being might be of a higher priority than my role as a submissive wife. So, I stood there in the doorway. Waiting.

"You know what the problem is?" His question struck me, although I knew it was rhetorical. Thick silence hung in the air, an avalanche waiting to crash down. I swallowed repeatedly, willing saliva to wet my dry mouth. "Let me tell you what the problem is. The problem is, *you thought*. No one cares what you think. No one cares what you have to say, what your ideas are, not one single thought that goes on inside that ugly little head of yours matters." One eyebrow raised, he looked at me, daring me to respond.

I blinked back the tears that threatened to accumulate. Crying would only make things worse.

"I'm not going to fight with you," my whispered words surprised my own ears as they escaped my lips. I was beyond being hurt by his insults. I couldn't do this anymore. Even the thought of where an argument would lead right now was more than I could stomach.

"What did you say?"

I stiffened. My spine extended, and I stood as tall as I was. I felt my shoulders drop. I spoke a little louder as I repeated myself, "I said, I'm not going to fight with you."

He laughed with a villainous sneer. I wondered what was coming.

Never had I spoken so simply and so directly to him before. Oh, I had questioned and I had begged more times than I could count. Pleaded for him to forgive me, love me, help me understand how to fix whatever I'd screwed up. All I wanted was a happy life, a godly marriage, a peaceful home and loving family. Each time he would tell me that if only I listened, if only I would do the things he told me to, try harder, stop making the same mistakes. But I had never put down a boundary, never told him I wouldn't participate.

"You don't get it do you? You're nothing! You never have been. A little girl from Arlington got herself pregnant and couldn't even finish high school. Ha! I did you a favor getting you pregnant. You never would have amounted to anything. You probably planned it. Didn't you? The smartest thing you ever did, get yourself knocked up so I'd have to marry you. No diploma. And those people you work for, they don't think you're smart. You know that, right?"

Don sat there shaking his head. He paused to let his words sink in. "Seriously? You can't possibly think they hired you because they think you are smart. They needed someone who could come in and answer the phones. Nothing more. You aren't intelligent enough to do anything other than that. You couldn't even finish high school. But you lied about that. What did you say on your application? Graduated, Arlington High School, Class of 1991? I wonder what would happen if they found out you didn't graduate. And you lied? Oh, I know, they'd fire your sorry ass. No more job. Then what? What would you do then? Nothing, that's what. No one else would hire you. You know that, right? Why? Because you're stupid, that's why."

Don waited for me to respond. Waited for me to speak, to say something in my defense. I knew better than to fall for the bait. It didn't end well for me when I did. Ten years of this never-ending cycle. Time between arguments getting shorter and the damage greater.

"I'm not going to argue with you." I let out a breath with the words. My tone erred on the side of pleading.

"Oh really? Is that so?"

Then a flash of our last big fight came to me. I saw myself on the floor covering my head. I couldn't let this escalate. "What do you want? What do you want from me?" I waved the white flag. Deep breath in.

"I want a divorce," he sneered at me.

A divorce? Divorce was a sin, of course, but if my husband was asking for a divorce, that had to count for something. Didn't it? I heard the key turn in the lock of the chains that bound me. My eyes popped open as I heard myself say, "You got it."

Alarm bells rang inside my head. I needed to go fast. My feet began to move before my mind could tell them to. I turned, leaving the room, no hesitation. This was a loophole for me. Even if leaving Don meant leaving God, even if I lost my soul, I had to go. Who was I to God or to Laurie if I was dead? Bolting through the living room and down the stairs to his office, I fumbled with the phone and dialed my mother's number.

She answered on the second ring, "Hello?"

"Mom? I need you to come get me. Now. If I don't leave tonight, I'll never leave. Can you come?" I was speaking quickly, my racing thoughts spilling out of my mouth, through the telephone line and into my mother's ear. Would she listen to my cry for help? Would she defy my husband in a way she had never defied my father? I desperately wanted her to tell me I was worth the risk.

"Okay, honey, we'll come, but it will take at least an hour. Where is he? Where is Laurie? Have you called the police?"

"He's in our room, sitting at the computer. He's calm right now. Thinks he's won an argument. Laurie is in her bedroom. She probably heard everything that was said. I'll go get her. He said he wants a divorce. Just come. Mom, please hurry."

"Okay. I'll call your brother and see if he can bring his truck. Promise me if he does anything you'll call 9-1-1. We're on our way, honey, be safe."

"I will Mom, I promise."

I rushed back upstairs to Laurie's room, grabbing a box of Hefty garbage bags on the way. I saw Don was still sitting at the computer in our bedroom as I passed by.

"Laurie, we're leaving tonight." She sat on her bed holding her teddy bear.

"Okay, Mom. Tell me what to do." An expectant look upon her face, her voice no more than a whisper.

"Put anything you want to take into these bags. Stay in your room with the door closed. Do NOT open the door for any reason. I will come back in a few minutes." Her body likely full of fear, the confidence on her face did not waiver as she moved to follow my instructions.

"Honey?" I paused at the door before I closed it.

"Yes Mommy?"

"It's going to be alright. Everything, you and me, we're going to be all right." My sweet girl nodded as a single tear escaped her strong fortress and trickled down her cheek.

I closed her bedroom door behind me. I was about to embark on the road to freedom.

A Bible verse came to mind as I began to gather things and take them downstairs where my mother and father would meet us. "If the Son therefore shall make you free, ye shall be free indeed." Just that. Freedom, if only the Son would make me free. I hoped He was in my husband's request for a divorce. No matter, I had to go. It was now or never.

Kristi Lyn Reddy, mother of two, married to the love of her and her children's life, is a soccer mom, writer, and real estate broker in Seattle. After beating cancer twice in 2016, she took up running with the motto, *'I run because I can.'* She has completed two 5K's, the Sounder's 9K, UW-Husky 10K, Seahawks 12K, and recently a 10-mile run for Soldiers with PTSD. Through her writing, she hopes to empower others to take a stand for themselves and others struggling to break free from the lingering effects of abuse. Her anthology piece is adapted from her developing memoir, *Uncovering the Warrior Within: Giving Way to Your Inner Voice.*

Close Call

By Ronna Russell

I was dreamin' when I wrote this
Forgive me if it goes astray
But when I woke up this mornin'
Could have sworn it was judgment day...
1999 Prince

I stood, disbelieving, as he shut the door to the garage behind him. Then I stood by the door listening to the car pull
out as the three of them left together. I kept standing there
as the automatic garage door whirred closed. We were in another new city in another new state, the third one in high school
alone. I was dazed by the heat of Sacramento, sweating in my
pantyhose and polyester, frizzy hair in a dowdy twist.

As soon as we'd settled in our new house, my older sister,
Karissa, had immediately begun dating the pastor's son and
had gotten a job in a travel agency. Dad and Mom went daily to
their jobs at the church as the new assistant pastor and secretary duo. And I had attempted to navigate the beginning of my
senior year at my new school, Del Campo High. Alone.

The day everyone drove away leaving me overnight in an
empty house in a strange new city was not long after school
started. Karissa had scored free tickets to Hawaii at the agency
and decided to take Mom along on a vacation. Dad had volun-
teered to drive them to the airport in San Francisco, a couple of
hours away, and I assumed I would come along. While Mom
and Karissa took their suitcases to the garage, leaving the door
open, I could hear them chattering and opening car doors. Then

I heard Dad pick up his keys.

I scurried to get a sweater from the closet in case it got chilly after dark. "Time to go?" I asked Dad, grabbing my purse as Mom and Karissa got in the car.

He turned to look at me with a surprised expression. "Oh, well…, you should just stay here, Ronna. It's a long drive and I'll stay overnight near the airport. I'll come home in the morning," he said decisively, though there was also something careful in his tone. "I'll see you tomorrow." He didn't stop moving as he spoke. I watched them drive away. That is how I found myself home alone on my eighteenth birthday, six weeks into a new town, knowing no one. I was surprised to be left completely alone on my birthday. Shocked, even. No one had asked me what I would do while home alone. There was no one to spend the evening with. I stood there numb with rejection. Inside the house, the blank white walls of my new bedroom stared back at me as I sat down on my bed. The emptiness and silence pulsed, suffocating me as they closed in. They'd left me.

I had a car, an orange Pinto wagon that ran most of the time, and I remembered the way to Casa Maria's Mexican Restaurant and Bar at Sunrise Mall. I was damned if I was going to sit in that house by myself, staring at the walls, on my birthday. Also, I hadn't had sex in the three years since Lance dumped me. No one had touched me since then and I was starving to be noticed and touched. None of the California boys in Dad's church were interested in me because I was too fat and still dressed like a Pentecostal. My need for contact boiled inside. My craving to be with someone ached.

At dusk, I drove my trembling Pinto down the wide, open streets to Casa Maria's and pulled into a vast, almost empty mall parking lot beneath a red neon sign with a flashing sombrero. Without hesitation, I parked and walked in the double wooden doors.

The bar was to the immediate left of the entrance. The bartender glanced up, but before he could speak, the only guy sitting at the bar looked me up and down.

"Come here," he said, with a motion of his head.

I walked over, trance-like, and slid onto a barstool beside him without a word. I didn't have a thought in my head.

The bartender looked a little nervous. "Do you have ID?"

"No," I said.

"Let's go," the guy on the barstool said. He was Hispanic, barely taller than me when we stood up, with bushy black hair and a thin, sparse mustache. At least 30, maybe older. I couldn't tell.

I followed him out, glancing back over my shoulder as we went, noting a look of shock on the bartender's face. Outside, the guy hopped into my car without any discussion. I followed his directions to another bar, but got carded again, so we left and cut to the chase.

We climbed in the back of my Pinto wagon, leaving the hatchback up. I slipped off my shoes and slid my underwear off. He had not told me his name nor did he ask mine. I hadn't spoken at all other than to admit that I was not 21.

"Turn over," he said, taking charge immediately. Then he pushed my skirt up and fucked me from behind. Right there in the parking lot as I stared out the back in silence. My mind detached and floated away as he entered me over and over. It didn't hurt. I couldn't feel anything. I heard his whispered groans as he pumped into me, faster and faster. I didn't want him there after a while, but I also didn't have any great urgency for him to finish.

After he finally came, I climbed out of the back of the Pinto, ducking to avoid the raised hatch and stood outside in the parking lot in the soft evening air. Felt the warm breeze on my face. I wouldn't have needed that sweater if I'd gone with Dad. I pulled my underwear on while the guy peed on the asphalt. I watched his steaming stream of urine flow underneath my shoes, an ugly beige mesh peep-toe flat with a bow on the toe. I knew I would never wear those shoes again.

I pulled the hatch down and got into the driver's seat as he climbed in the other side so I could drive him back to his car in the Casa Maria parking lot. We still didn't speak.

At the parking lot, he said, "My name is Louie, don't forget," he called to me as he drove off, his music blaring through the window. "Tonight we're gonna party like it's 1999..." Prince's voice trailed behind as his sports car accelerated and sped away.

I went straight home, navigating the ten minute drive in a daze. Back in my bedroom, I stared numbly at the undecorated walls. The whole encounter hadn't even taken an hour, and I was still very much alone on my birthday. I didn't inspect my body or take a shower or think about why I had walked out my door and had sex with the first stranger I saw. Nothing. I just crawled into bed, curled up around myself and drifted off to sleep in the silence.

Dad arrived home the next afternoon. I heard the car door slam. Then another door. Someone was with him. The front door burst open. I left my room and went into the living room to greet him.

"Surprise! Look who's here!" Dad announced in a sing-song voice. Jesse, Dad's friend from Portland, followed him in, suitcase in hand. His black skin gleamed in the sunlight streaming in around them. Dad knew Jesse from church. I knew him too, but I didn't know they were good enough friends for us to host him at our house.

"Heyyy, girl! Look who's here! How are youuuu?" Jesse asked with his familiar smirk as he reached toward me with a one armed, halfhearted hug.

"Umm, hi, fine, how're you?" I tried not to act surprised at his presence. No one tells me anything, I thought. I turned around and went back into my room.

That night, the three of us went to dinner at a sidewalk café, and I carefully perched in a white wrought iron chair as I picked at my food. As if somehow this arrangement was normal—dinner alone with dad and Jesse. Dad never explained why he was here with us. At the end of the evening, Jesse walked right into my parent's bedroom and shut the door. I hadn't noticed where his suitcase had been put. Is that where he was going to sleep?

I watched as the door closed behind him, leaving Dad to face me in the hallway.

"Isn't Jesse going to stay in Karissa's room?" I asked in shock.

That was my parents' bedroom. The master bedroom. Where my parents slept together every night. I wasn't even allowed in there. Why did Jesse get to sleep in there? Was Dad going to sleep in there too? Or was he taking Karissa's bed?

We were both poised as if for flight outside our respective bedroom doors, each eager to disappear behind them.

Then Dad said this, "You know, it's just like when you have a friend over." His tone was conciliatory as he turned away. *You understand*, the tone said, *we're going to stay up late and gossip, maybe do each other's hair*. Then he opened his bedroom door and took a step to move in.

"Oh," I nodded and stepped into my bedroom, shutting the door behind me. I tried not to imagine what was happening behind the other door. My heart pounded.

The three of us went to church together on Sunday morning. Dad presented Jesse as a guest singer. He stood up in front of the congregation and sang as everyone worshipped, as if he had every right to be there.

Mom called to check in that afternoon.

"Jesse's here," I mentioned.

"What?" she choked. "When did he get there?" By her tone I could tell she clearly hadn't known he would be coming.

"Right after you left," I answered.

"Let me talk to your dad," she snapped.

I didn't know what was going on. Except I did.

If my mom thought she had problems, I had a problem of my own brewing that night too.

Back in the 1980s, pregnancy tests were only available at doctor's offices, nothing of the kind was sold over the counter. I didn't have a doctor or any money. Within days of my self-inflicted sex collision, I was panicked, and secretly searched the yellow pages for pregnancy clinics then scoured the accompanying city maps to see if I knew how to get to them. I was new here and Sacramento was huge; webs of streets stretched for pages of indecipherable blurry grids. Finally, I saw an ad for a free pregnancy test at a nearby church. I made an appointment for 1:00 the next afternoon even though I hadn't yet missed a period.

Mom was home from Hawaii. I'd never heard her and Dad talk about Jesse and I never asked. On a Tuesday, I told her I wasn't feeling well and stayed home from school. I peed in a cup but could not keep it refrigerated, as instructed on the phone, so I hid it in my closet. I worried that room temperature pee wouldn't work for the test, but a cup of pee in the refrigerator would be noticed. I decided to take a chance. At 12:45, I told

Mom I was feeling miraculously better and that I would go to the library but instead quickly slipped out the garage door with my cup of urine tucked in a brown paper lunch bag and stuffed into my purse.

As the garage door clanked open, I turned to see a heavily made-up Asian woman standing on the sidewalk. A bandana covered her hair, she wore false eyelashes, thick black eyeliner and blue eyeshadow. I don't know where she came from, maybe a visitor to one of the neighbor's houses. I'd never seen her before, but I nodded at her and tried to walk past.

"You know what means the word slut?" she said, accusingly.

I panicked, opened my eyes wide and looked behind me to make sure my mother wasn't in earshot. "No," I said. Then I whirled around and dove into my car, slamming the door shut. *Who was she? How did she know?* I wondered. I had to get out of there.

I turned the key, revved the sputtering engine and backed the Pinto out of the driveway as fast as I could, looking around frantically as I reversed into the street. The woman was gone. Not on the sidewalk, not in a neighboring yard. Vanished. Had she been a hallucination? Sent to accuse me?

I found the church and the clinic, turned in my pee cup to the woman behind the counter and was told that in exchange for the information I sought, I was required to watch an anti-abortion film. It would take two hours. Of course there was a catch! It was a free clinic. I settled into a folding chair at the end of an empty row, alone in a dark, cool room. As soon as the film started, I realized I had seen it before in youth group.

"I've seen this film before," I said, sticking my head out the door.

"Oh, ok, well... your test results were negative, however it's too soon to really know for sure," she said with concern. "You could still be pregnant."

I nodded. I knew it was true.

"Would you have an abortion if it turns out you are pregnant?" she asked, as if another option existed.

"Yes," I said and walked out into the glaring sunlight.

Almost a week later, before Wednesday evening Bible study, I leaned against the church's bathroom cubicle wall as twisting cramps contorted my body. I slid down the cold metal to a squat, silently sobbing and trying to breathe, the intensity of the pain driving all coherent thought from my head. I could barely see straight, much less wonder what was happening. After a few minutes, the pains subsided enough for me stand up and catch my breath, clutching the top of the toilet paper dispenser. I had never felt anything like that before. The pain was similar to period cramps but times a million and with knives. I fled the church building and drove home, sweating and shaking. Mom was on her way out the door to go to service when I got there. I explained I wasn't feeling well—the only excuse to forgive the cardinal sin of missing a church service—and went straight to bed.

Pain yanked me awake hours later, in the middle of the night. The cramps had returned with a vengeance. Pain seared and rocked my body so violently that I could feel it in my chest. I called out to Mom for help. Mom called Dad, who was out of town, to ask what to do. I heard her low worried voice on the phone. He instructed her to take me to the nearest emergency room in Roseville.

I don't remember the drive or checking in. No questions, no exams, no x-rays later, I was sent home with possible pneumonia and told to lay low for a couple of days.

A day later, the cramps began again with terrifying force. Dad was back in town by then. I called him at work.

"I need you to come get me, come quick. Please," I begged, my terror clear.

And he did.

Dad took me to a walk-in clinic on Sunrise Avenue, not too far from Casa Maria's where I'd met the guy in the bar. There were questions and x-rays this time. And a moment alone with the doctor.

"Is there a chance you might be pregnant?" he asked tactfully.

I nodded silently, relieved. Finally, someone had asked the right question.

The doctor told Dad to take me back to the emergency room immediately and he did. I was still in my tattered lime green sweats that I always wore to bed. I knew going to the emergency room had something to do with the doctor's question, but had no idea what. My mind had started to blank again.

I sat in a padded vinyl chair in the imaging area of the hospital, waiting for my name to be called. Dad sat in the chair beside me, leaning forward, inspecting his fingernails, his jaw clenched.

"Is this the first time you had sex?" he asked tersely, not looking at me.

"No," I whispered. "Remember Lance?" My breath caught on his name as my heart jumped with fear.

Dad's jaw rippled with anger now. He cleared his throat and pulled his fingernail clippers out of his pocket and began to clean his nails. He didn't say anything else but his rage settled into the air around us.

I leaned back, resting my head on the sticky plastic, heart and lungs vying for space. Fear of the repercussions that would come after this medical emergency was over vibrated through my body.

Now he knew. I wasn't a virgin and hadn't been for a long time. I had done a terrible thing more than once and had gotten myself into real trouble this time. I was being inconvenient again. What would he do to me after this x-ray thing was over? His silent fury overwhelmed any concern for myself. Whatever was happening inside my body was secondary.

Someone called my name. I do not remember following them into the changing room or what they said after that. I swerved onto the bench, unable to approach the folded white cotton robe beside me on the bench. Mirrors and hooks began a discombobulated swirl as my head spun. *I think I am supposed to put that on*, I thought.

The ultrasound technician came in to see if I was ready, but I could no longer stand or respond. She helped me up and onto a table in the adjacent room, placed a cold instrument on my lower abdomen and turned to watch the screen. Instantly, she was on the phone, urgency in her voice; words I could not decipher. Her voice sounded far away. She looked far away, too, even though she must have been standing right beside me.

Moments later, gurney wheeling down a hallway, voices yelling, operating room, bright lights, scissor blades ripped through lime green terry cloth, masked faces loomed...

"Count backwards..."

"100, 99, 98..."

Recovery room. Slide from the gurney to the bed. Really?

The ultrasound technician stood at the foot of my bed, pale and shaken, surprised I had survived. I remember the metal staples marching across my lower abdomen, a forever scar.

The nurse said, "You're gonna use birth control next time, aren't ya?" as she wiped me down with a wet sponge. My cheeks burned with humiliation.

"Yeah," I whispered into the pillow while she rubbed my ass.

"Your fallopian tube ruptured. It's called an ectopic pregnancy. You lost so much blood you're lucky to be alive," she noted briskly as she hoisted the scrub tub under her arm and walked out.

Dad stopped by the hospital once during my week-long stay. He perched on the edge of my bed and read scriptures out loud and prayed. Karissa came to see me every day after work, but Mom didn't come. No one mentioned Mom to me and I did not ask where she was or if she knew what happened. I was relieved to not have to face her shock and disappointment.

No one discussed what had happened that night or asked who got me pregnant. No one asked me why or how I felt or what they could do or what I needed. No one yelled or cried. There was no conversation, just a big fat Holy Shit atmosphere.

What I didn't know was that Dad had the family in communication lockdown—as he did about his own secret life as well. That's what he did. He locked us down. Karissa was forbidden to talk to Mom or anyone else about my pregnancy. She was allowed to come to the hospital to see me, but Mom was not. Karissa thought that Mom didn't know why I was hospitalized, because that is what Dad told her. I never attempted to talk to anyone about the experience; it was too shameful and I knew I didn't deserve comfort or forgiveness and I sure as hell didn't want to hear another Bible verse. My scream for help was met with silence.

In the weeks and months to come I floated away inside my head. My desperate reach for connection had backfired and I had been punished. It was my own fault. Silent days surrounded me like a prison cell. No one spoke to me. I heard no voices.

This terrible thing happened to me
I did this terrible thing
My body is broken
I am broken

Please talk to me
Don't talk to me
Would it have been easier if I had died?
Would it?

A few weeks later, we finally talked. Dad sat at the head of the dining room table, papers spread before him. The medical bills had arrived.

"Brother Adams had to backdate the insurance paperwork to get this thing covered," he said as he cleared his throat and straightened papers into stacks. "We have a $3,000 deductible. I think it's only fair that you pay it."

"Okay," I murmured.

"How much can you pay per month?" he asked, his mouth set.

"$150? I'll get a job," I promised.

"Mm. Okay." he accepted, returning his attention to the stacks.

Something had been bothering me, though. What happened would not have happened if I'd been taken seriously during the first trip to the hospital. And my father was a stickler for justice. "Dad?" I said cautiously, "Umm, I'm just wondering why you aren't suing the hospital for negligence, for sending me home with a diagnosis of pneumonia?" I felt tremulous.

"I would have, if something had happened. It was a close call," he said.

The silence that ensued pounded in my ears. There could be no more complete proof of my personal irrelevance than that it did not matter if I died beyond how he would handle the bills. Solid evidence that my emotional and physical state were of importance to no one.

When I look back at all of this now, I am not quite sure how I survived or if I did. What part of myself vanished during that time?

Six weeks absent from my senior year, no one noticed when I went back to school. I had been a new face, anyway. I limped through my senior year, heavy with heartbreak, going along with the fabricated appendicitis story Dad told the church people.

Not long after, Dad was caught in a gay bathhouse and secretly fired from the church. A story was concocted for the congregation, a vague decision to relocate for work, his resignation letter read from the pulpit after Dad had already moved to L.A. The same story was told to us all, including my mother. No one told my mother why her husband no longer had a job as assistant pastor, even though she was still the church secretary. No one told her that he was caught with his dick in a glory-hole or whatever. Dad certainly didn't tell her. He just left. I knew.

Dad found work selling insurance in L.A. and Jesse from Portland joined him there. Mom was mostly left alone, trying to make ends meet. One evening, she and I were sitting on her bed discussing my apparent lack of devotion to church.

"I noticed when I did the books that you aren't paying tithes," she began. "Where is Christ in your life? Your father and I..."

"Mom, Dad is gay," I interrupted. "Jesse slept in your bed with Dad while you and Karissa were in Hawaii."

Her face froze. "He stayed in our room?"

"Yes, Mom. And now they live together. How long has it been since he slept with you?" I asked.

"Not that long," she snapped angrily.

"Then you should probably be tested for AIDS," I said, bluntly, and walked out, tired of the silence. Tired of being the wayward one.

Decades later, a therapist told me, "Find a picture of that teenage girl, from around the time of the tubal pregnancy, when you were alone and your family fractured. Every morning, look at her and say, 'You're with me. I've got you and we are going to get through this.' "

I did it. I found a picture of myself that I could hardly stand to look at. It was taken at the lake with my family, right after I had taken a futile SAT test. I drove to meet them for a picnic in a panic, crying and pleading to God all way, please don't let me be pregnant, please don't let me be pregnant. Knowing I was, but with no idea what was coming. The young woman in the picture is hungover, fat, scared and miserable and about to have a life-threatening event.

Every morning for a month, I reached for that picture and gave her a good look until she met my eyes.

"You're with me," I said. "All day. I'm going to take care of you."

This self-compassion got easier as the days went by. We both started to believe I could take care of her. Somehow during that month, I began to look at that miserable girl in the photo with empathy, instead of shame and hatred. I pulled her toward me through the years, the first time she had ever not been pushed away. And I listened to her. Neither of us is silenced anymore.

Ronna Russell grew up the youngest of three daughters born to a Pentecostal preacher. The mandates of the United Pentecostal Church never set well with Ronna, and from an early age, she plotted to get out as soon as possible, hell or no hell. She jumped into marriage at the age of twenty-three, a union that lasted 22 years and produced four children. When the marriage ended, she worked several jobs to support her children as well as face the choices she made that led to this precarious place. Ronna also found that she was free to consider her own desires and to write about her experiences. With these transitions behind her and her children grown, Ronna has relocated, remarried, and returned to school.

Bright Lights, Booming Sounds

By Priscilla Sharrow

Seven years after the accident that resulted in my traumatic brain injury—when a man's case fell out of an overhead bin on an airplane and landed directly on my head—my son was getting married in San Francisco.

I am one of those traditional mothers who counted the days until Marcus would marry so I could proudly glide around the dance floor in his strong arms as he towered over me at six feet. A mom deserves—after breastfeeding a tiny preemie baby every two hours, years of messy diapers, Cub Scout and Boy Scout meetings, fundraisers, and many school projects—to reap this coveted place in front of family and friends. I had earned such an honored place in this transitional time of his life. I was excited as I anticipated all the wedding festivities.

Marcus had chosen a Chinese-American woman as his bride and helpmate, so on the wedding day, although Marcus and Tina would ultimately live in Seattle, I found myself in downtown San Francisco in the middle of Chinatown at a famous restaurant booked by my future-in-laws. Tina and her family were not the warm, fuzzy types. Hugs were somewhat nonexistent. Family traditions were set in stone. Our family cultures clashed like the sound of two cymbals meeting each other in mid-air. I am French–Canadian, while my son's Dad is Mexican. The differences between my family and Tina's family hit me in the face the moment I walked upstairs to the dining room where hours of dining, drinking, and dancing would occur. The large circular room was segregated by table arrangements with Marcus' family and friends on one side and Tina's family and friends off to the other side, with a large bare area for division. I was seated at the head table with the bride, bridegroom, and the bride's parents and grandparents. Tina was dressed in a traditional Chinese red dress with a slit up the side. She had changed out of her white bridal dress that she'd worn at the Presbyterian Church ceremony. After a formal Chinese dinner was served, Tina changed into her third wedding dress, a long, plum-colored brocade dress for the evening's dance.

Ah! Excitement and emotion began to take over my thoughts as Marcus held Tina in his arms for the Newlywed's Slow Dance. Soon to follow would be the moment for the Mother/Son dance, right after the Father/Daughter dance. I waited, but never saw Tina's Dad approach her for the next dance, and Marcus never looked my way either. I felt concerned that these traditional dances I'd anticipated were not going to happen after all. What was wrong? I would let it pass, of course, but I was disappointed. Terribly so.

Then suddenly, before I'd processed that the order of events was not what I'd been expecting, "Kaboom! Kaboom!" the large speakers in the hall began to resound with pop music—very loud and vibrating in the room.

"Let's give it out to Marcus and Tina, Mr. and Mrs. Marcus Najera," bellowed out the hired DJ, Rick. Colored strobe lights began to blink as the young guests took to the dance floor.

Nausea gripped me as my head began to swirl.

Fireworks were exploding in my injured brain.

The music was way too loud for my injured brain. I needed to ask Marcus to lower the volume of the music booming out of the speakers. I felt embarrassed to ask him. Marcus was a Top 40 Music personality, well-known and loved in the Bay Area. Music was his life and this was his wedding. What right did I have to ask him to lower the volume of the music? Everyone seemed to be enjoying it even though the music tortured me. But I wouldn't even get a mid-reception dance in with him if this nausea took over. My equilibrium had never righted itself since the accident.

Agitated and frightened, panic and disorientation flooded my body.

I needed get away from this music NOW! I went to find my newlywed son.

"How are you doing, Mom?" he said when I found him. "Sorry I couldn't dance with you, but Tina wouldn't allow me to do it since she didn't want to dance with her father."

I let him know I was disappointed, but understood. Tina's parents had been divorced when she was young, and she had a strained relationship with her Dad. I could see the awkwardness of the situation. Our conversation continued over the booming music.

"Hey, Marcus!"

"Yeah, Mom."

"Can you please turn the music down a little? It is too loud for me."

"Oh, Mom, I can't turn down the music, the dancing is getting started."

Then someone interrupted us, so he had to leave quickly in the direction of his bride.

Sad and frustrated, I made my way back to find a new place to sit at the crowded tables. Soon I had a headache. Seated next to my best friend now, I closed my eyes. Noelle immediately recognized symptoms I had previously exhibited at a noisy event we attended together. I told her what Marcus had said.

"Priscilla, let me get you out of here," Noelle insisted. "The loud music and colored lights are not good for you. If Marcus can't lower the music, then we need to leave NOW!"

I didn't want to leave the wedding. Heartbreak filled my chest, but I could feel my symptoms worsening. "Ok, let's go," I answered reluctantly. I grabbed my black sweater coat and followed her downstairs to the busy street below. We headed for her car, parked six blocks away. It was a dark, chilly night with a slight foggy breeze coming off the Pacific Ocean, blanketing San Francisco. I wrapped my coat around my tense body and pulled it close up to my chin. I began to shiver and take quick breaths, trying to calm myself. Salty tears rolled down my cheeks. I had left my son's wedding reception early. I'd had no time to say goodbye to anyone. I was in a survival mode. A sad moment in time.

Soon I slid into the back seat of Noelle's forest green BMW sedan, buckled myself in loosely, and stretched out the best I could. My head was spinning and my brain hurt. I fell asleep while Noelle drove us to the Marriott Suites, twenty miles away.

When we arrived, she shook me gently.

"Wake up, Priscilla," she said. "We are at the hotel."

Although still a little disoriented, I felt rested and calm again. A slight headache still throbbed as I made my way to the elevator. Arriving at my room, I bid Noelle goodnight and slept well until a morning phone call woke me up.

"Hello, Mom," said a familiar voice. "It's Marcus."

"Hi, how are you this morning?"

"I am a little upset. Why did you leave the reception last night early? You never said goodbye. You and Noelle just disappeared. I looked all over the room for you. Where did you go? Were you disappointed because I didn't dance with you? I argued with Tina about that before the wedding, but just finally gave up. I am so sorry, Mom. I really wanted to dance with you."

I sensed a deep sadness and remorse in his voice as I struggled to find loving words to respond. I, too, was disappointed, saddened, and embarrassed. What should I say? The reality of the situation was so much more than a lost wedding dance tradition. My sadness ran deeper than that. I'd missed most of my son's special night.

Grabbing a Kleenex, I wiped the tears from my eyes. Slowly I spoke from my heart.

"Marcus, yes, I was very disappointed and confused when you didn't approach me to lead me to the dance floor," I replied trying to keep my voice steady. "But when I didn't see Tina and her father dancing, I figured it just wasn't a Chinese tradition. Then the volume and type of music changed. I didn't realize the booming sounds and blinking strobe lights would cause my brain so much agitation. I felt nauseous." I took a breath.

He was quiet on the phone. "I am so sorry. I was so embarrassed but I had to escape the sounds in a hurry. I had no time to search you out again. Noelle realized I was in trouble, so she whisked me away to her car. Then she drove me to the hotel."

"Mom, I am so sorry," said Marcus. I could hear the regret in Marcus' voice as he choked back tears. "I didn't realize what the music was doing to you. How can I make it up to you now? How are you feeling this morning?"

"I am feeling fine this morning, but really sad we didn't have the dance. It was a tradition I anticipated your entire life—to dance at your wedding. It's a lost moment for me, to be honest." I wasn't trying to make him feel guilty, but Marcus and I had always been truthful with each other. "I'll be driving home right after breakfast. Have a wonderful honeymoon with Tina. Maybe I can come for a visit to Seattle in a few months when you get all settled down in your condo."

"Can we meet down in the lobby in about an hour to say goodbye?" Marcus quickly responded.

We met in the hotel lobby to say our parting words. I hugged my "little boy," now a grown man at thirty-one, who had crossed the threshold into married life. I was proud of the awesome and caring man he had become.

Two months later, special friends of Marcus and Tina from the Radio Broadcasting World hosted a celebration dinner in honor of their marriage in Seattle. I traveled to attend. The event was a glitzy night complete with champagne, a four-course dinner, and dancing in one of Lake Washington's popular restaurants. Little did I know, Marcus had special plans for us that evening. When the dancing was to begin, he took the microphone and announced it was now time for our Mother/Son Dance. He walked to my table, lifted my hand into his, and led me to the dance floor. He then requested the DJ to play his favorite song, dedicated to his Mother: "A song for Mama" sung by Boyz II   Men. The music began. Not too loud. As he held me in his arms, our eyes met.

"Mama, this is for you," he softly said with tender emotion. "I hope it makes up for what we didn't have at the wedding. Forgive me. I love you."

"I forgive you and I love you so very much," I managed to say as I smiled through my tears of joy and love. "Thank you for this honor and dance." I had regained a special memory that I thought would be lost forever—The Wedding Dance with my son, Marcus Daniel.

Priscilla Sharrow, a California native and a Northwest transplant since 2005, now resides in Bellingham, Washington with husband, Cliff and fur baby, Jacques, a lively labradoodle. She is a lover of adventures, a storyteller of life experiences, and the writer of "Messages from the Heart," a newsletter portraying spiritual messages with words and photos, offering wisdom and wit on every page. In progress: *Bonked!* her memoir about her traumatic brain injury.

Searching for Levity

By Kathie Tupper

I've just moved into my own small space, a first floor apartment in someone else's house only big enough for two cats and me. At age fifty-two, I've moved out of my latest boyfriend's house after a twenty-month trial run, ending my forty-seventh relationship since sixth grade, including two husbands. I'm pumped to have my own space, but I'm also anxious. I am finally ready to face a serious, lifelong fear of being alone, and I don't want to engage my dormant eating disorder which always threatens resurgence whenever I have a breakup or even think about living alone. A week in, I'm feeling strong. My question about whether I will finally become that strong, powerful, independent woman so many people in my life think I am begins to fade. But on the eighth day, I wake up and have a sudden urge to buy a new bathroom scale. My former boyfriend had been obsessed with daily weigh-ins, a habit I fully embraced for our months of living together. My weight hovered between 120 and 125 during that time, an acceptable number for me on my five-foot seven-inch frame, so I never relapsed into bingeing and purging while we were together. It takes consistent semi-vigorous exercise to keep my weight there, and I'm tired of watching the number so closely. I want to *not* need a scale, but admittedly I feel dependent—I am afraid if I don't monitor my weight, it will somehow get out of control. I'm addicted to weighing myself, among other things.

In my defense, I was born and raised in an addictive environment, starting when Mom took potentially lethal doses of barbiturates while I was *in utero*. She had developed an incredibly high tolerance for sedatives, and the amount of secobarbital combined with meprobomate she took was enough to kill most people—but not her, or me. I was bound to learn to cope with life through excess.

At my highest weight outside of pregnancies, I felt constantly bloated, embarrassed to be seen, like I was not living in my own skin. When I look at the rare picture of myself from that time, I cringe in self-loathing—I looked like a chipmunk storing up for winter with swollen glands in my neck and swelling in my face and jaw from perpetual self-induced vomiting. My self-esteem was literally and figuratively in the toilet. Psychologically I never want to go to that place again, so I weigh myself. It doesn't matter that my highest weight was still a healthy weight for someone of my height. It doesn't matter that a scale can't actually stop me from bingeing and purging. But logic doesn't matter in the matter of Kathie vs. Her Body.

I give in and bring a new digital scale home, put in the batteries, and prepare to weigh myself the following morning.

Morning comes, and I am nervous. Naked, I step gently on the scale. It screams at me, "134!"

"Holy Shit!" I shout so loudly the cats scramble. "I've gained over ten pounds in two weeks!" I start to sweat. I step off the scale. Then I step on again, thinking it's registered wrong, hoping the number will magically drop. It doesn't. I repeat this—off and back on again—several times. "It's just a fucking number," I say, finally walking away from the scale in disgust.

I dress for the day, feeling heavy, discouraged, and generally crappy about myself—and hating that this number—134—can make me feel worthless.

As I drive to my job as a massage therapist, I think about that number. Until it glared red at me, I hadn't *felt* any bigger, but now I see my protruding stomach poking up against the seatbelt. As I walk from my car to my office, I feel my thighs brush against each other. I want to shield my body from others. To hide.

Later that day a male client who has just stretched out on the table comments to me, "You look good. Have you gained weight?" I freeze. A wave of panic pounds at my heart.

"Maybe," I answer. "I don't really know." It's nobody's business what I weigh or don't, and it pisses me off that people notice or care. Or that I care. Or that I care that people care. I keep my tortured thinking to myself.

Experts recommend that folks recovering from eating disorders should weigh themselves no more than once a week. But of course I can't wait that long. Obsessive fear is taking up too much space in my brain, and I can't stand it for long. Two mornings later, I prepare to weigh myself again. With a sudden flash of optimism, I have an idea. Maybe, just maybe, the floor is uneven! If so, the scale wouldn't give me a fair reading, would it?

I take the scale to a different part of my living space, right by my bed. It's a Pergo floor, not tile like the bathroom. That should be flat. Anxiously, I step on. Here, the number reads 119! I breathe an audible sigh of relief. "Oh, thank God!" I get off and on again. Same number. So I was right. Either the floor is uneven or I have lost a bunch of weight in the last forty-eight hours. I have to know which, so I move the scale all around the apartment, weighing myself here and there. 123 here, 114 there. I even pick up each of the cats and weigh them with me since I know their body weights.

The whole thing is ridiculous, and after ten minutes of this, I'm able to laugh at myself. The cats are looking at me like I'm crazy. I know what they mean. A naked woman holding her cats on a scale! Good thing the curtains are still closed, or I'd get a strange reputation among my new neighbors. A new lightness and ease waves over me, and somehow today my clothes magically fit better. My stomach is flatter too. I delight in the new, lighter me.

Later that day, a long-time client comments, "You look good...even tinier than usual."

You have no idea how that statement fucks with my head, I think. But I just get her on the table, and we spend the massage enjoying easy, lighthearted conversation while I work out her tight muscles.

Everything about me has lightened up by the end of the day, and I desperately want the feeling to last, for time to suspend in this space of levity. I'm reminded that nothing means anything unless I give it meaning. I vow to remember that a number on the scale is just that—a number, not an indictment of how unworthy of love I am. And an offhand comment is just an observation, not a proclamation of truth about my value. I've spent over thirty years making negative meanings about my weight, and frankly, I'm exhausted by it. I've got to keep taking tentative steps on toward self-acceptance. And I have a plan.

My twenty-six year-old daughter, Shannon, comes over the next day to help me unpack. Organization is not my forte, but it is Shannon's, and I need her direction. I have avoided going through all my crap for the past seventeen years, but now I feel an urgency to purge my material chaos, let go of what has kept me stuck. Maybe *this* is the kind of purging I really need to undertake.

Today, we are focusing on box upon box of my old journals. These journals are a monster reminder of my messed-up history, and I'm afraid to look. I stand in my bedroom next to the pile of notebooks stalling for time, leaning against the dresser, as Shannon gets us organized. She's sitting on my bed, surrounded by boxes, and I really look at her for a moment. She's shorter than me, five-foot four-inches to my five-foot seven-inches. I notice that her body is rounder and more pear-shaped than mine, but that she seems content with herself. I hope so. I don't want her to suffer like I have. I desperately want to open up conversation on this topic with her. I want to know if she escaped my demons, but I'm not sure how to do it, so I don't.

Instead I sit on the bed across from her and turn my attention to the journals. I pick up one and thumb through. Then another. The word "Insomnia" pops off page after page. "I'm just like Grandma!" I comment to Shannon with alarm. "She spent her whole life obsessing about never being able to sleep." Maybe being born addicted to sleeping pills has something to do with that in my case.

I flip through another journal. Another theme, of course, is trying not to binge, doing it anyway, regretting it, starting over after a period of bingeing—year after year after year. Relationship troubles jump off the pages, too—the importance I place on how I feel about myself based on who I am with, feelings of neediness, devastation and failure when I inevitably leave, elation when I fall in love again. Then alcohol, the times I drank after vowing not to. Regret, then commitment to turn over a new leaf...so similar to the dysfunctional eating. I cringe as I read, shrinking into the comforter. "Wow!" I say to Shannon. "Maybe I shouldn't read all of these!"

"You shouldn't." She says simply, as she looks at me. Curious, consoling. How much does she know, I wonder?

I look away from Shannon's questioning glance, back to the journals. "I think that's good enough for now." I finally say. "Let's take a break."

Together we place the journals in plastic bins and shove the monster under the bed.

"Well at least I will have lots of food for thought on my hike!" I say.

Shannon and her brother, my son Kyle, know about my intended solo backpack trip of the 220-mile John Muir Trail, less than five months away. They don't know that I've devised this trip to face my fear of being alone *and* to take some serious steps toward self-acceptance and healing. Alone in the woods for a long hike is how I plan to find love for myself while avoiding all possibility of indulging in any of my various addictions.

I know Shannon is worried about my doing this. She says so. But then she says, "Mom, I know you are going to do what you are going to do. I know it means a lot to you. I'm sure it will be a great experience." I desperately want and need her approval, and THAT, I realize, may be the best trip endorsement I get from her.

A couple more weeks of Shannon and organizing, and I am all settled in. I turn my energy to preparations for solo backpacking. Before I can undertake my massive quest, I need surgery to remove some hardware from my right foot. The procedure is scheduled for the first week of May, so I decide to go for one more good and challenging epic training hike before that happens.

I ask my twenty-three year-old son, Kyle, to join me. He's fit, fast, and ambitious. We've chosen Mt. Si for our hike, an hour or so from Seattle. It's the last Saturday in April, the sun is out, and the forecast calls for highs in the seventies. A perfect day with perfect conditions, but as I wait in line for the stinky, overused and under-cleaned trailhead bathrooms, I am nervous. Suddenly I feel older and worried about my psychological make-up. I don't doubt my physical capability to do today's hike with Kyle or even to take on the John Muir Trail in three months. But I do wonder if I can handle all my various addictive tendencies that will have to come along too.

"Ready to roll, mom?" Kyle asks when we have both used the facilities and there is no more stalling to be had. "Here, let me carry some stuff. I'll take your lunch. You might as well carry a light pack while you can!"

"Yep, let's do it," I say. "How about this, Kyle. You go first, set the pace, and if I can't keep up with you, I will let you know. But I wouldn't mind being pushed a bit on this hike. Sound like a plan?"

He turns around and smiles. "OK, you got it Mom." And we're off.

At first, I struggle. I am breathing harder than I normally do, and trying not to let that show. It's my pride, I know, but I don't want to appear weak. I'm focusing on putting one foot (and alternating pole) in front of the next when I have an epiphany; that's really the problem in all of my life, isn't it? I don't want to appear all kinds of things: weak, fat, incompetent, sad.

I reflect on this thought as Kyle and I sail past everybody! I won't be feeling weak today, that's for sure. I feel exhilarated instead. Our brisk pace makes me feel young, powerful, and strong. Like magic, my body finds a rhythm. *This* is the kind of high I most want and crave. The fresh air and movement of my body through it bring joy, period. But this hard pace also keeps me right at the edge of what my physical body can handle, and dancing on that fine line between healthy exercise and obsession. Even here, I play with addiction.

I let Kyle talk as we go, so I can focus on breathing. He tells me of his feelings about starting graduate school for physical therapy in Georgia, and of the challenges and excitement of beginning such a big adventure so far away from home. My heart is bursting with pride and beating with exertion when we finally reach the top.

We find a spot and plop down, overlooking the valley below, and Mt. Rainier off in the distance. Suddenly, I am filled with emotion. Both my kids seem so together. More so than I am. They are my offspring but they are both so healthy in a multitude of ways. Both have emotional equilibrium that still eludes me and have already found long-term partners. Each has embarked on a sustainable career path inspired by passion. They astound me. Maybe in spite of myself, I've done some things well enough to allow them their own happiness.

"Kyle," I say, fighting back tears. "I am proud of you and Shannon for the people you have become. How did you both turn out so well?"

He looks at me sideways. "Ah, Mom. You're silly. Of course we turned out fine. We had you as our mom, didn't we?"

In that moment, on top of Mt. Si, I vow to be for them what Kyle thinks I already am. Healthy and whole, and mostly, honest in my relationship with them. I never had that with my Mom, and the sadness of that threatens to overwhelm me further. My kids inspire me to be the best version of myself I can be. And that means finding self-love in a radical way that includes all of my previous failures and all of my flaws.

On our way back down the mountain, again with Kyle in front of me, I know my solo trek on the John Muir Trail will be a quest for peace. Immersion in nature, being alone, and digging deep into resources I don't yet know I have will lead me, gently, away from the recriminating numbers on scales and accusing words in decades of journals.

Kathie Tupper is a Health and Life Coach, Massage Therapist, and avid outdoor enthusiast. She details her path to finding inner peace and healing through her upcoming memoir, *No Crutches for This Mountain Goat*. She loves to share her passion for overcoming obstacles, reframing disadvantageous patterns of thinking, and cultivating self-love and acceptance by spending time in nature.

Rivers and Ashes

By Jacquelyn Lenox Tuxill

My parents, both doctors, stated in their wills what they wanted done with their remains. The single sentence conveys so well who they were.

I hereby direct that my remains be cremated, and that the ashes therefrom be preserved until, with the ashes of my spouse John/Cora, they be sprinkled into the waters of the Tygarts Valley River in West Virginia, eventually to mingle symbolically in infinitesimal amounts with global waters and thereby signify my feeling of identity with peoples of all nations and races, and the hope for a worldwide family of nations with justice and peace for all.

Two things characterized my parents' life together: medicine and China. They were married in September 1930 in Mom's hometown in South Carolina. Their union did not begin on an auspicious note as her father opposed their marriage and refused to attend the simple ceremony held in his own home. My grandfather was being his cantankerous self, furious that a Yankee had stolen his favorite daughter from under his thumb.

They started their marriage as medical missionaries in China. Upon arriving at West China Union University in Chengdu, they studied the language for two years. Then Dad began teaching medicine in Chinese and Mom joined a small class of eight other medical students, three men and five women. She graduated in 1936 and worked full-time until we three children were born at two-year intervals beginning in 1940:

Marilyn, then I, then Don. She worked some after Marilyn and I were born, but the war with Japan soon changed that.

With war overtaking China's eastern provinces, universities relocated to campuses farther west, several to Chengdu. When Japanese fighter planes brought the war to Chengdu, my parents had to worry about air raids and getting babies safely into bomb shelters. So we fled Chengdu for America in 1944 when I was two-and-a-half years old, eventually settling in rural West Virginia where I grew up. When the Communists assumed control in 1949, the door slammed shut on the life and work my parents had loved, and they lost all communication with their Chinese friends for many years.

Dad died in 1996, and my siblings and I kept his ashes safe until he and Mom could be joined again in death. She passed away three years later, on the day of her weekly lecture to medical students, a job she would never agree to retire from. After her memorial service my siblings and I plan a trip to West Virginia to honor the request stated in their wills.

The summer day is warm and sunny when Marilyn, Don and his wife Carol, and my parents' longtime caregiver Jeri and her husband Joe, and I meet at the overlook above the town where I grew up. It's been years since I've been back here. Dad had loved this view of the river and the railroad winding through town. The poignancy of the occasion lends a somber note to our greetings, but there's an air of celebration too. We're about to launch our parents on a grand journey that echoes their honeymoon to China in 1930.

I broach an idea that I've been considering. "I'd like to reserve a portion of Dad and Mom's ashes to take back to China. I'll be returning at some point." When I was a child I had been mortified whenever my parents spoke Chinese in public. Our home was filled with mementoes from China and my parents often gave talks about their time in China. I'd resented these ties because they made me feel so different from my friends. But then I took a trip to Chengdu with Mom and Dad in 1980 after China reopened to Westerners. Thirty-eight by then and more curious than resentful, I'd witnessed their emotional reunion with their friends. That trip helped me better understand the deep affinity they felt for China, and I found myself drawn to the country of my birth.

"Where are you thinking to scatter their ashes?" Don asks.

"Places important to them like Mt. Omei, where they spent their first summer, and their campsite opposite the Minya Gongka in Tibet. They probably never dreamed of such an opportunity. I don't think they'd be opposed, do you?"

"I think they'd love it," Marilyn says as the others nod.

We leave the overlook, drive into town, and turn onto a dirt road along the river. I realize with a flash that Dad taught me to drive on this road. The river appears shallow with a sluggish current and muddy banks. I remember it as being much bigger. How will we ever get their ashes into the center of the river to the better current?

We drive along slowly, scouting along the bank for a good spot. Up ahead Don sticks his arm out and points to a small spit extending into the water. We get out of our cars. The spit, just big enough for one person, seems our best option. After a moment of silent good-byes, Don carries the container of ashes onto the spit. I imagine their ashes weaving through freshwaters, wending toward the ocean. That's when I realize there is a problem with my parents' wishes as written in their will. They hadn't looked at the geography.

"Hey," I call, "Dad and Mom are never going to global waters from this spit. There are dams between here and the Gulf of Mexico."

Don, halfway out, turns, nods, and walks back. We huddle and decide to go ahead and honor their request to be let go here anyway. Don walks to the end of the spit, takes a handful of ashes, and flings them as far as he can. But there's no breeze. I watch the ashes drift down into the water not far from his feet and sink to the bottom in a whitish-gray blob.

"How long before ashes dissolve?" I ask Marilyn. "Will Mom and Dad just become part of the bottom muck?" We're both horrified, but it also strikes us as rather funny. None of us envisioned this when imagining the ceremony of spreading their ashes. Not even you, Mom and Dad.

Don throws several more handfuls and eventually some ashes begin to move downstream a bit. But a mound remains conspicuously just off the spit. What can we do?

In the end he scatters only a third of their ashes in the river and I become guardian of the rest for my trip to China.

We walk back to our cars and Don and Carol say good-bye while the rest of us drive back to Pittsburgh where Marilyn and I are staying with Jeri and Joe. That evening we go out to a Chinese restaurant, pull up two extra chairs, and request six sets of chopsticks. We order Mom's favorite dish of *hui guo ru* (twice cooked pork) and have a delicious, laughter-filled evening of reminiscing. I convince Jeri and Joe to drive the next day with Marilyn and me back to Vermont so we can extend our visit before Marilyn flies home to the west coast.

On our way to Vermont, we decide to visit Bucknell University, Dad's alma mater, in Lewisburg, Pennsylvania. In all my trips to Pittsburgh when Dad or Mom were sick, there seemed never enough time to stop. Next visit, I'd say, as I passed the Lewisburg exit. Today we poke around the campus for an hour and find the older quadrangle of buildings that had been Dad's college. Sitting on nearby benches we become silly, imagining Dad, the jokester, as a young college student.

As we leave Lewisburg, we cross the Susquehanna River and an idea pops into my head. Are you prompting me, Dad? I pull to the side of the road after the bridge and turn the ignition off.

"We're going to give Mom and Dad another chance to reach global waters," I announce.

Chesapeake Bay—open water—is not far downstream. There may be dams between Lewisburg and the bay but far fewer than on the Ohio and Mississippi. We walk halfway across the big iron bridge and look out, high above the river. There's a good breeze and the Susquehanna flows wide and deep, the current strong.

"This looks perfect: a double-pronged strategy to get Mom and Dad to the ocean," I say, then to Jeri, "You want to do the honors?"

"You bet." The sparkle in her eyes speaks her love for my parents. She launches ashes and as they drift downward and away on the wind, two butterflies flutter up from below the bridge.

Marilyn looks at me. "Dad and Mom just gave their blessing," she says as we hug.

Several years pass as I study Chinese and transcribe the voluminous letters my parents wrote to their families from China.

Through the transcription process I see how extraordinary their life there had been, not only their work and their friendships with the Chinese—students and faculty alike—but also the community of missionaries from three countries and five denominations. I come to understand that Dad saw their wedding as the opening act of a grand adventure together—which it was, beginning with a three-month honeymoon halfway around the world. He had completed his medical training and been given a post by the American Baptist Foreign Mission Board to teach at West China Union University. Mom had finished one year of medical school and was determined to continue her studies in China. She was going to be a doctor too, come hell or high water.

The newlyweds left South Carolina by train and headed north to Canada then west through the autumn-cloaked Canadian Rockies to Vancouver, British Columbia. A month-long voyage followed across the Pacific Ocean. They reached Shanghai in early November but were still only halfway to Chengdu. Many weeks of upriver travel followed, starting with sailing up the Yangzi River aboard an armored steamboat. After evading Communist gunfire from shore at one point, the pilot safely negotiated the treacherous rocks and rapids of the Yangzi River gorges. They left the Yangzi at the confluence with the Min River, changing to a smaller river junk and the centuries-old means of travel—twelve men pulled them upriver to Chengdu. Arriving just before Christmas, they were welcomed by the campus missionaries with fireworks.

As the transcription process continues, I keep my eyes open for an opportunity to return to China. Finally, a travel guide friend tells me she will lead a tour in spring 2005 that will include a boat trip down the Yangzi gorges. Perfect. I couldn't resist the opportunity—Dad's account from 1930 had captivated me:

The river wound crookedly between mountains rising abruptly two thousand feet above the river, some sheer precipices overhanging the boat as if they would topple onto us at any moment. Rock strata of various colors ran in three or four different directions, often twisted and whorled. Hitting a rapid, the undercurrents and force of the water set the boat rolling almost as on the ocean, the bow inundated by muddy water beaten into a yellow-

ish spray. To the side were miniature waterfalls and many back currents and whirlpools.

Who wouldn't want to see all of that beauty? As I prepare for the trip, I know my experience will be different from my parents'. The new Three Gorges Dam sits just below the gorges, and for two years a reservoir has been rising behind it, already inundating the rapids and turbulent waters. But do you miss what you've never experienced? The dramatic setting—narrow gorges, steep mountains, temples perched on ridges—will still be there.

My parents are on my mind as I pack. They'd always been my bridge to understanding China, my go-to sources when I had questions. I feel your loss immensely, Mom and Dad. I tuck a small red pouch of ashes into my luggage. But you're coming with me, and you're always in my heart.

When I get to China, I feel the deep connection to the culture and landscapes that I'd felt on my previous trip. The Yangzi boat trip, the midpoint in our itinerary, will begin in Chongqing. We fly into a brand-new airport and, as the tour bus takes us toward the city, industrial cranes are everywhere. Block after block of concrete high-rises are under construction, the density mind-boggling. Are these office buildings? Apartments for the one million people displaced by the rising reservoir?

Mom and Dad, you wouldn't recognize it. I pat the place in my carry-on where their ashes live for the moment. Occasionally I see flashes of green—remnant farmland—and once a small wooden building of traditional design. I crave these scenes from an earlier time because they connect me to a China that is familiar from my parents' photos and stories.

When it is nearly time for us to sail, I walk the short path to the pontoon where several Yangzi cruise boats wait and remember my parents' description from 1930. They'd climbed hundreds of steps from the river to the city wall, steps that were slippery from men carrying water into the city. Chongqing was known for those steps. All that my parents wrote about in their letters is gone, torn down or covered by the reservoir. I feel sad for what has been lost.

We depart at dusk as the lights of the city blink on. Over the next several days, I keep to myself, thinking and observing. I didn't intend to be antisocial, but I joined this trip for very personal reasons and want to wring every bit of meaning from the experience. I visit with tour-mates over meals but stay on deck for long stretches, heedless of chill and damp and wind. When I do go inside it seems as if I'm in some plush Western bubble, separated from the China slipping silently by outside—a China I yearn to absorb into my every pore.

At regular intervals, signs with numbers march up from the river's edge. The highest marker—175 meters (574 feet)—is the reservoir's expected height when full. The water stands at the three-quarters mark. The slopes below 175 meters are mostly barren except for weeds and trash. The old towns and cities have been replaced by new concrete cities at higher elevations. Occasionally waters lap at fields where ramshackle houses and tangerine trees stand. Here farmers continue tending the land, stubbornly waiting for the rising water to drive them away.

Not everything has been sacrificed to the reservoir. Some temples were disassembled for reconstruction elsewhere. A few temples near the high water mark await a protective retaining wall. We dock at one such place: Shibaozhai, a twelve-story red pavilion built against a cliff face to provide access to the temple on top. When the boat docks, I walk the brief distance to the entrance and climb steep stairs to a round "moon" window with a view of the river and small farms nearby. I look down at the path that ambles amid mud and weeds to our boat. A few temporary food and souvenir booths hold forth for tourists, all that remains of the ancient river town.

During those days on the Yangzi I take photograph after photograph of the beauty that remains, wishing I could have seen it in 1930. Oh, Mom and Dad, the river dragon has indeed been tamed. The bustling river towns are gone. The natural beauty of the gorges remains but, strangely, for this wilderness-lover, without people it seems sterile. My heart aches for the farmers and the elderly who had to leave the Yangzi, the only life they'd known, for a China that is fast changing—the world of high-rises.

Dad wrote about the difficult life along the river—at best a constant struggle to eke out a bare living, at worst life-threatening, especially for the countless men who had toiled over the centuries before steam power to pull the junks upriver through the gorges. I can imagine that difficulty, but the way of life had been unique, evolving in an intimate spiritual relationship with the Yangzi. Would today's experience inspire reverence and poetry as it did through the centuries before technology?

Throughout my time in the gorges I try to comprehend how being born in China defines me. No longer a tourist, I seek the China of my birth as a context for understanding what I see and experience here. The glimpses of an earlier time always resonate, always feel more authentic to me than today's concrete cities that seem at first glance to have more in common with western cities.

I finally realize that I carry that earlier China within me. A baby bird imprints on the first thing it sees, usually the mother, and that first image triggers identity and bonding. In a similar sense my earliest memories, my first attempts at language that enable me to speak Chinese with a Chengdu accent—and more that lies buried—are all part of the visceral essence of who I am. Dad and Mom, how I wish I could talk with you about this.

On the last evening aboard ship, I climb to the top deck, relieved to find myself alone. Tomorrow we pass through the lock at the Three Gorges Dam. The breeze contrasts with the stuffy lounge below and the waning moon plays hide-and-seek with scudding clouds. I can just make out the dramatic mountain shapes floating by as the boat, engines rumbling, moves along the quiet water of the reservoir.

Taking the red pouch from my pocket, I walk to the stern to catch the wind. The moon is suddenly clear of clouds as I grasp a handful of weightless ashes. With tears rolling down my cheeks, I lift my hand and let the ashes stream back in the wind.

"You're back in China, Mom and Dad, together forever in this beautiful place. My love goes with you."

Jacquelyn Lenox Tuxill has authored numerous reports and handbooks during thirty years of environmental work, including a dozen publications while she was a partner with the National Park Service Conservation Study Institute. She splits her time between Lincoln, Vermont, and Bellingham, Washington. Her essay, "Rivers and Ashes," is adapted from her forthcoming memoir, *Whispers from the Valley of the Yak.*

The Three Dollar Bridge

By Kate Voorhees

Buzz, Carl, and Shmitty would be there at the cabin of course. In their first year in college Buzz and my dad went fly-fishing in Colorado. The following year when they planned to repeat the trip, my dad suggested they should get some of their other "bros" to join them. Buzz said, "Forget about those guys," but my dad invited them anyway. There were five or six guys my dad's age who were part of the crew over the years. But Buzz, Carl and Shmitty were always there.

They fished in Colorado and Alaska and other places originally, but West Yellowstone and various rivers in the southwest corner of Montana became their passion. They loved to return year after year. At first, they only took one week a year, always in September. Then they extended into two weeks, and then three. My dad was the biggest advocate for extending the duration of the trip until ultimately in the final year they stayed a month. My dad and his bros had been ritualistic about their annual fishing trip for three decades by the time I was invited to join them.

I drove out of Jackson after work at the newspaper feeling a little stressed. I'd had trouble with the computer and had sat in front of it for ten hours completing the classified pages for the deadline. I didn't feel like getting into the jeep and driving two hours from Jackson to West Yellowstone through the park. Selfish. What was two hours in the grand scheme of things? Nothing.

The jeep climbed out of town past the elk refuge, and after only ten minutes of driving I felt better as the expansive views of the Teton Range began to emerge next to the unfolding highway. All I needed was to hit the open road in one of the most beautiful places in the country. U.S. 191 ran north out of Jackson through Teton Park. The Teton Range to the west of the highway served as the backdrop for the sunset, and a soft pink alpine glow of light illuminated the Gros Ventre Range to the east. The setting sun behind the jagged Teton Mountains cast luminous and dramatic shadows on the valley floor. There was no better place than here at this moment. This place was my backyard. I'd learned to live and play here, developing a healthy relationship with the mountains and rivers.

The speed limit was 45 mph, and I loved that. That was fast enough for me. It was September and the days were getting shorter as the calendar crept into the blanket of winter. The road was dark and it was late in the season, so there were more chances that I would run into an animal than a tourist.

When I arrived in West Yellowstone, I called the cabin at the Pine Shadows Motel from a pay phone. My father's good friend Shmitty answered the phone. "Hi Kate, I'm glad you made it safely. We are all here waiting for you," he relayed excitedly.

Shmitty and my dad met in college and had been bros for at least three decades. He grew up with my mom and knew her from high school. Shmitty claims responsibility for introducing the two in college, therefore being the reason that I existed. Shmitty told me in a letter before this trip that he would be my net if I ever needed one. He cared so much for my dad that he would do anything for him.

"Your dad is really looking forward to seeing you." he continued.

He gave me directions to the cabin and we hung up. The bros always stayed at a cabin on the property of the Pine Shadows Motel for their annual fishing trip. I got back into the jeep and wound through the small sleepy streets of West Yellowstone, arriving five minutes later with a tinge of anxiety.

Dad was there with the others, and when I saw him, my mom's words from our phone call the night before echoed back to me. "I don't see how he could possibly lose more weight." She had been with him every day since his diagnosis. I'd seen him infrequently, but every time I had been with him, I could see he was different. He was fading away physically. The cancer was eating his body.

What I didn't know then was that the day before my arrival, my dad received a call from a specialist doctor on the east coast, saying that he couldn't take my dad's case. This was detrimental information and depleted any hope he had of getting better.

That evening we all sat together talking. When it started to snow, my dad got quiet and stared out the window. Silent tears ran down his cheeks as Shmitty moved over to sit with him and scratch his back. They loved to scratch each other's backs.

The following day, at breakfast, my dad said to all of us, "I really appreciate you coming up here. It means a lot to me. I don't know how many more times we will get to do this."

That day Dad and I floated the Madison River with Blaine Heaps, the owner of the Pine Shadows and the best fly-fishing guide they knew. It was a crisp and clear autumn day. The mountains were light brown and yellow and jutted up from the valley the river meandered through. The water was an emerald green color and shallow and rocky in places.

As we fished, Dad said, "When I die," and he paused for a long time.

I gave a delayed, "Uh huh," even though I didn't want to hear about him dying.

"I want my ashes spread here on the Madison River at the Wade Lake Bridge."

We bobbed down the river under the bridge, which was otherwise known as the "*Three Dollar*," aptly nicknamed because the old farmer who lived up the road from the bridge charged anglers $3.00 to park at the bridge if they wanted to fish the river.

The sign he put up read:

> ATTENTION-FISHERMEN. THIS IS PRIVATE PROPERTY. A PARKING FEE OF $3.00 PER VEHICLE A DAY IS CHARGED. PLEASE DEPOSIT THE FEE WITH YOUR AUTO LICENSE NO.# ON THE ENVELOPES PROVIDED IN THE COLLECTION BOX. OVER NITE CAMPING $5.00. NONE PAYERS WILL BE BAND. WE THANK YOU FOR YOUR COOPERATION. THE MANAGEMENT.

What was most disturbing to me about my dad's illness was how he was like a child or a fragile elderly person. We had to help him take off his waders, untie his boots, and pull them off. He needed help with his vest, his jackets, and bags. He wore five layers of clothes to stay warm. He was so weak and skinny. I grieved hard for him—and for me—though he wasn't gone yet. Death, I thought, might seem like relief from this terrible illness.

These were my last real significant experiences with my dad in a conscious state. Fishing and floating in a skiff down the Madison River in Montana, just north of West Yellowstone, on a perfect autumn day in September 2000. I was twenty-six, and we didn't know at the time that Dad would not make his 57th birthday that November.

Two weeks later in mid-October I received the dreaded call from my mother.

"Your dad is in the intensive care. He may not make it, and you better come home."

I fell to the floor in the kitchen and wept and remained down there on the hard vinyl until I could shed no more tears and began to get cold and uncomfortable. I had to get it together and buy a ticket home. I had never taken a plane out of Jackson because the flights were expensive, but this time I couldn't be frugal. When I arrived at the airport, I was asked if I would be willing to get bumped to a different flight on a later date, and I nearly broke into tears. That question seemed like such an insult in the wake of what was happening with my dad.

I said no, got my boarding pass and waited to get on the plane. Sitting in the terminal I felt anger rise inside me. I was suddenly mad at my mother for not letting me know the severity of Dad's condition earlier. In an attempt to be optimistic, they kept me in the dark about how fast things were progressing. But then again, I wasn't there to see it with my own eyes either. How was it fair for me to be angry?

When I got to the hospital, my dad was on a morphine drip, and he was not talking or opening his eyes. My sister was there, and my mom and her sister, one of my dad's sisters, his mom, and all of the bros. Shmitty gave me a hug when I walked in. We all stood around staring at Dad and at each other. After a while, everybody scattered, and I was in the room alone with my mom and dad. She pulled the covers down to reveal my dad's torso to me. He was skin and bones. His rib cage protruded from the hollow cavity of his abdomen. I'm not really sure why she did that but the image of his emaciated body never left me.

Mom left the room, and I was alone with my dad. I felt uncomfortable; the room was stuffy as I sat there in silence. There was so much to say but the words would not come to me. I wanted to believe that even though he was under the influence of the morphine, and not outwardly conscious, he knew we were all there, and that he could hear and understand everything. There was something I should say. I should be more affectionate or something. Anything but the awful silence and the oppressive heaviness in the room.

Grief pushed in on me and made me feel like my back would break with the weight of it. Finally, I blurted, "I love you," and I ran out of the room.

My mom and my sister and I went back to my parents' house.

My dad passed away that night. He was not alone. My mom's sister was a nurse, not on duty, but she stayed. And the bros were there. A part of me thinks that my dad waited for us, his girls, to leave the room to die, like he was trying to protect us. The bros said they were waiting for us to leave so they could all fart. That was so like the bros to bring in humor in light of the inevitable end of a beautiful life.

But my biggest regret for years would be leaving that room that night.

Just shy of one year later we all met in West Yellowstone to spread Dad's ashes on the Madison River like he requested. The bros had received word that there was extensive reconstruction of the *Three Dollar* bridge that crossed the Madison River. The bros had always fly-fished the south banks of the river, which required crossing the bridge from the highway, which could now not be done. I think they actually wanted to take the long drive, but we did have to get to the other side somehow.

There was a network of rough gravelly backroads that eventually landed us on the south side of the river. We took the long road mostly in silence, reflecting on our own thoughts. We joked about how Dad probably ordered up the bridge remodel forcing us to take the long way; to appreciate the place where we were going rather than just arriving without properly reflecting on the nature of our visit. He did have an ornery side to him, which he mostly only let shine amongst the company of his bros.

The Madison River's headwaters are in West Yellowstone, near the junction of the Firehole River. From there, the waters meander east out of the park and eventually under the *Three Dollar Bridge,* where we spread his ashes.

Ashes to the Madison

I stand over the Madison River in Montana
On the *Three Dollar Bridge*
A year has passed
You are at peace now
Reunited with the river.

I think about you
Watching me
In amazement

You asked that I do the best I can
At whatever I choose.

I want to learn
From your spirit,
Your example.
You were strong
A fighter till your last breath

I loved watching thunderstorms
Warm and secure in your presence
I miss fishing with you.

My memories come
In pieces
I release you through them.

At first, he traveled north, braiding through the valley between the Madison and Gravelly Range. In a small Montana town called Three Forks, he combined forces with the Jefferson and Gallatin River, to form the mighty Missouri River. The Missouri River fearlessly carved him east through Montana and halfway into North Dakota, before he hooked south, through South Dakota. He floated the state line between Nebraska and Iowa, as well as the northeast corner of Kansas. Finally, he made it back to the place of his birth, in Kansas City, where the Kansas River joined the Missouri, and he tirelessly slogged east, desiring ultimately to return to the sea, which eventually the Mississippi River would converge with.

I am Kate Voorhees. I have a nagging call to unravel the tapestry of my history and weave the threads of memory back together with deeper understanding. That, and I like the feeling of the keys on my fingertips, making magic, as letters become words, and words create sentences. I create sketches composed of words and document snippets of conversations, observations, and shared moments. I am an adventurer, a builder, and a creator. My writing is a response to the call from that tapestry.

Job Satisfaction

By Wendy Welch

I hate the library, fucking hate it. I've worked in this building since 1967. Practically lived in the place. I used to live for it. The glue they use in new books? I could smell that, told the girls there was fresh stock in the workroom before they even opened the boxes. And that musty smell from old books, the ones in the glass cases in reference you couldn't take out? I used to open the cases at night, after the lights went off, and just breathe air tinged with antique book perfume.

How sad is that?

Nowadays we circulate reference books. The policy handbook says so. "In the 21st century, the librarian's role is not to be poised as a medieval dragon atop the treasure horde of knowledge, but to throw open the gates of a well-organised garden of public information." Some smart-ass twenty-something got a First on her thesis for that shite.

A whiff of glue today and it won't be long before some pseudo-student rips out the bar code and sneaks out the door with a £30 book. We'll find it advertised on E-bay a week later. There aren't any real students anymore, no kids seriously looking to learn. Just cyberpunks.

Welcome to the library. That's me, behind the counter. Oh wait, you blinked, now I'm stocking shelves. Whoops, there's trouble in the Family Learning Centre, somebody's trying to view porn on one of our 42 shiny new state-of-the-art, Bill-Gates-donated PCs, and the library administrator will be coming down from her Ivory Office any minute. Mustn't let her see that, or several trees will die in the resulting memo flurry. Okay, crisis averted, dear little learner was sent off with a stern warning about Revoked Privileges, screen was cleared just as the old biddy emerged from the elevator. Smile.

"Good morning, Ms. Low. How was the conference in Dublin?" *The one you promised I could go to, ya two-faced harpy.* "Yes, I'm remembering, 2 o'clock; I'll have them in by then." *Aye, I'll have the circulation statistics in. All the way in, ya sodding...*

Back to the shelves. Take books from the trolley, find the right place. Shove them onto the lovely new faux-obsidian finish. It's so slick the hardbacks keep going, sliding straight out the back onto the floor unless you jam them together with some spare part of your of anatomy until you can wrestle those godforsaken magnetic bookends into position.

Somebody was thinking clearly about that shelving. (That's sarcasm, dears.) I can write you the script. Upstairs, where half of them have never been to Library College, someone opened a catalogue on her big oak desk. "This one looks nice," she said, and set us on the slippery faux-obsidian path to Hell.

Not long after those monstrosities arrived, Father James came in—there's six of us here goes to St. Matthews. He's not known for having spare time to read, that saint of a man, so of course I went running over, "Hello Father, was there something you wanted, Father? What can I help you find?" And he said no, thank you, he just wanted to see the "black monoliths of Satan" for himself.

I think he was joking?

Did you know, stocking shelves is why we librarians wear our glasses on chains? Once I did a knee jam on a waist-high shelf, pinioned the little bastards with the bookend, got more off the cart and elbowed them into place, then turned to find three teenagers grinning at me. "The Russian judge gives it a 7," one said. Cheeky monkeys.

Stocking shelves is a bitch. Crime and horror and science fiction are easy, by the author's last name. Any literate cow off the street could do it, and finding literate cows is so much easier than finding literate students. But see that bloody "Mind Body Spirit" section? That's what the enlightened call the combined categories of Religion, Food and Exercise now that we're a trendy, cutting-edge facility. Recipes for carrot cake in with the Torah. Once I put a book called "Cooking with Oranges" next to a biography on Pope John Paul. Just try keeping the

"Mind Body Spirit" books Dewey decimalised. All I can say is, the punters into that stuff must love chaos theory. In the morning those books are lined up neat and straight as soldiers in the Army of The Lord, and by 7 p.m. the 001.994s are in the 356.2s.

You don't care, do you? You just yawned, admit it. What's important about organising books, after all? Who gets their knickers in a twist if the numbers are backward, or Fredericks gets in front of Forest? The Public.

God help us all, The Public come to the library looking for something to hate. Wearing good shoes and carrying rolled-up umbrellas, they enter this vault of knowledge to read up on The Bad Guys. Ready to get the Real Secret Facts on an epoch of history. Surfing the council website for evidence that the local MP is soft on homosexuality. Scouring for dirt on every page.

Don't tell me people come in here to gain knowledge. They come for ammunition.

So if the ammo happens to be ass-backward for a month of Sundays because Lending Staff are sharing 'round a spectacularly virulent strain of flu virus, The Public turn on the librarians. They've come here to shoot, and they're not particularly fussy about targets.

Heaven forfend that the college kids from Administration should help us actually keep the library going if the flu descends. No no, the clever young employees hired by the 21st century Library Board are here to Develop New Approaches, not hand out printed reading matter or answer questions for The Public.

Once I took one of those little clicker counters, you know, the kind that you use at the market, and every time The Public asked me a question, I clicked it. Guess how many, at the end of a nine-hour shift? 246. I took it to Admin and they said, "Why were you counting people with that? We have better methods than a hand-clicker. Next time, ask us for the stats."

So help me God, if one more Letter to the Editor complains that the books are a mess and the staff all surly, I will personally force-feed all 312 pages of the policy handbook to the next Yuppie graduate who waltzes down the stairs with "a wonderful idea for an innovative programme that will attract new users to the library." Hey kids, here's a brilliant and untried plan: let's try keeping up with the users that are in the effing place already.

I had just started here when the library added the new wing in 1967. Princess Margaret cut the ribbon. Lending was all on one floor then. Eight months later, during The Troubles, some arse threw a stone through the back window of Children's and lobbed in a Molotov cocktail. I can close my eyes and see it like it was this morning. A little girl with blond braids done up in red ribbons, standing next to a turn rack of easy readers, screaming as the window glass burst, and that bottle whooshing in like a butterfly of death. Well, didn't I catch the damn thing and throw it back out the window? Didn't even think. And THWOOOP! It went off in the alley.

I got a letter from the Head of Cultural Services, and the newspaper took my picture. That little girl is an Infants teacher now. She brings her class in here every September for a Welcome Tour. I don't know if she remembers the bottle. I never ask her.

We got a computerised booking system in 1984; Sarah and Ken and I joked about that for months. 1984, like the Orwell book, get it? Oh never mind.

The computerized system doesn't help much with The Public. They still come up, lean on the counter, and blow their bad breath at us, asking "Where's Steven King, luv?"

Sarah used to answer, "Maine, but I can call him if you like. He's a personal friend."

Sweet saints, how I miss Sarah and Ken Sullivan. They were here when God was a boy. Ken died in the staff room, eleven years ago come September. Stroke. Sarah tried to resuscitate him until the paramedics came. He was declared dead when they arrived at the hospital.

Sarah retired in 2010. We still eat lunch together on Fridays, down on High Street.

Big Brother—that's what we called the useless computer system—was supposed to keep track of who took out what. Two years it took to get "the bugs" out, and those tech-boys in shirt sleeves and one earring kept coming in, punching the keyboard a few times, saying things like, "There you go, pet. Never have another minute's bother from this. It'll make everything faster once you learn to use it! Big change, but we mustn't be afraid of this new technology. It's just what you used to do on paper."

"Pet." I don't know which is worse, that or thinking I'm too intimidated to push buttons on a keyboard. Or to count the staff time that piece of shite ate—not to mention a big chunk of the budget—calling out the Earring Brigade. I learned everything there was to know about that system, training on my own, just to show them. Staring at me in my twin set as if I were a relic of antiquity. I showed those lads it's true: You can't judge a book by its cover. Since '87, I've trained every new library assistant on that fucking system. And I watch the money fly through those PCs, the black holes of the library, again in 2012 when they "upgraded" and we went down the rabbit hole again.

A woman used to come in here Saturdays, like clockwork just after 10. She'd ask every single time, did we have any new authors in? Always had a list of the latest bestsellers, which ones did we have, could she reserve them if they weren't here. We called her the Novel Lady.

She drove me crazy, so diminutive and predictable, did we have any new authors, did we have any new bestsellers, until one day when I was the only one on the counter and the line stretching back to the stairwell, I lost it. I looked her straight in the eyes and said, "D'ya think our budget comes straight from the Queen, that we get money for new books every day? Why don't you try the bookstore, if you want the latest?"

Well, she burst into tears. I felt so bad (snarling at The Public, me!) that I got Mags to work the counter and took her to the staff room for a cuppa. Ann—that was her name—had her husband at home. He was hurt on the factory floor but his company wouldn't pay for care, even though it was their fault. She had to leave her job at the hospital to be his nurse. Her daughter came on Saturdays to give her half a day to herself. That's why she was at the library: to get books for the week. I cried so hard, she ended up comforting me.

Ann kept coming right up until 1996. Her husband died in—let's see, it was after the Family Learning Centre got the computers, anyway. Then she died of cancer, but she'd remarried. Nice bloke. Younger. He still comes in. Ann and I used to give each other sweets at Christmas.

People. It used to be about people. Divide The Public into little bits, and you could find real people. Now it's all beeping from infrared checkout scans and computers powering up and that sodding music playing over the loudspeakers. And you can tell me that I'm past my sell-by date, but The Public don't divide down anymore. They're just a big lump of the same old demands. Ammunition.

And lately they talk to me as if I were a book from Special Collections. (Sarah and I used to do afterhours there, wiping the old things down with spirits solution to protect them.)

When we finished, she'd always say, "'If these books were people, they'd be confused, hard of hearing, and incontinent. You know, some old people still have all their accumulated knowledge locked up in their own brains, but no one can get to it. And others do just fine. When we're old, let's not wind up in Special Collections."

And I'd always answer, "We are old." Then we'd go for drinks.

Special Collections is another bit they did away with in their New and Impressive Library wisdom. The books have been "stored," the library administrator said when I asked. "And it's not your job to worry about these things."

Bitch. She doesn't have to tell me my job; I was here back when she was blowing money and boys in university. It's my job to worry about porn on the computer screens and clearing used condoms from the lavies, and "other duties as assigned." For instance, that memorable night when, making the rounds for closing, I uncovered a new library assistant in the broom closet with a lad, taking the experiential approach to literature. I got her transferred because every day after that she'd look at me with her big grey eyes full of fear; it was just a matter of time before she realised I wasn't going to turn her in and did it again, and she was a screamer.

But I've done a few turns in the stacks myself. This generation think they invented sex. I didn't always wear knit suits and loafers; I had my days in the sun. The last one was only five years ago. We took a few books off the shelves that night, let me tell you. Stick that in your collective earlobes, tech-boys!

The Public wouldn't believe it. Grey hair, glasses, sensible shoes, plump: one must be the sum of one's parts. The Public don't know everything about where my parts have been. Their minds aren't open enough to let in that kind of information.

The Public talk to me like this: "Ah, you'll have seen some changes yourself, Miss Mumphrey. A lifetime in the library! And you and I know that all this new-fangled technology can't take away the human touch, can it now?" And pat me on the arm like a stray kitten. Their little town mascot. Patronising sods.

And yet.... I wouldn't say so to them, but I'll tell you, since we won't be seeing each other again. What they say takes some of the sting out of the printed words, the ones inside the envelope in my pocket. Printed on the dark space behind my eyelids when I scrunch them shut to avoid the words.

"Dear Miss Mumphrey, What an honour it is to thank you for forty-seven years of devoted service to the council as a {lending staff} with {insert department} The Central Library. As you know, unless in cases of senior management, council policy does not permit employment past an individual's 68th birthday. This letter is to invite yourself and a colleague chosen by you to a luncheon with your head of department, honouring your life's work...".

It goes on a bit like that.

I hate the library. Fucking hate it. Stinking new glue. Ungrateful self-important users. I hate it all. Hate it, hate it, hate it...

Wendy Welch is an ethnographer and bookstore owner from Virginia. Her previous books are *The Little Bookstore of Big Stone Gap*, *Fall or Fly: The Strangely Hopeful Story of Foster Care and Adoption in Appalachia*, *Puddledub to Paradise*, and *Public Health in Appalachia*. Wendy heads a cat rescue called *Appalachian Feline Friends* and loves to crochet, swim, and read.

God and Movies and Love and Me

By Jennifer Wilke

Sundays were heavenly to me when I was growing up. My dad wasn't busy working, my mom wasn't busy cleaning or volunteering, and they weren't out together square dancing, playing cards with their friends, or going to a dress-up party. On Sundays, I didn't have to stay home alone doing my homework, practicing the piano, reading, playing with our beloved cocker spaniel Honey, or watching TV. On Sundays, my parents and I spent the whole day together doing fun things, like going on picnics or hikes, or visiting friends with a cabin on Flathead Lake where we could swim. We'd always go to the county fair and the circus when it came to town, and once we went to a rodeo! In bad weather or winter, we might stay home and work on a 1,000-piece jigsaw puzzle, or play Monopoly, or go ice skating at the indoor rink, or on the lake when it froze. A few times my dad and I complained when my mom insisted we go to a museum, but it turned out to be fascinating to learn about the history of the whole world and everything in it. On that trip, I stared up in wide-eyed silence at the skeleton of a giraffe for so long that my folks made a joke that they would have to kidnap me away to get me to stop gawking.

On our Sundays together, we'd often get home tired and happy, eat supper, and then watch TV together. When *The Ed Sullivan Show* ended, I knew I had to go to bed. Snuggling under the blankets on a Sunday night after all day with my parents is how love felt to me—warm and safe.

One sunny and sparkling Sunday morning in winter when I was eight years old, Mom and Dad and I drove to First Presbyterian Church, the way we always started our Sundays. I wore my black patent leather shoes with white ankle socks, a favorite dress, and a green wool coat Mom had sewn for me, with satin lining and brass buttons—an exact match to the coat she had made for herself and wore today too. I stood tall, proud of being a fashion plate beside my mother, paying attention to the people who smiled in approval when they saw us. The walk from the car to the church made the end of my nose chilly, but my hands were warm. My dad had taken my right hand in his big, rougher one, and my mom reached for my left hand with her smooth, lotioned one. Holding their hands, I felt anchored and safe, walking together up the stone steps toward the massive church doors where God lived. Of course, I couldn't know that my sureness in that every-Sunday scene, my hands in theirs, came from the hidden truth that I was the one anchoring both of them, helping their relationship endure.

The sermon that Sunday morning was penance I had to pay in advance for the exciting outing to come as soon as the minister stopped talking. I occupied myself by trying to remember the Ten Commandments we'd studied in Sunday School. There were eight Don'ts: Don't worship or make an idol of any god except God (that was two don'ts), don't say bad things about God, don't murder anybody, don't steal anybody's husband or wife, and don't steal things that belong to other people. Don't tell a lie about anybody, and don't envy what they have. There were only two simpler, Do's: do keep the Sabbath day holy, and do honor your father and your mother. "Sabbath" meant Sunday. I hoped God would understand that the only day my parents and I could see a movie together was on Sunday. This movie was *about* the Bible, so it should be allowed on the Sabbath.

Mom put her hand on my leg to stop my impatient jiggling. I pulled up Dad's shirt cuff to check the time on his wristwatch.

"Don't worry. We won't be late," he whispered, one eyebrow rising as he pulled his cuff down. He put his arm around my shoulder, and I leaned against his side, glad of the comfort even though he didn't understand how many things I was worried about. The newspaper said there'd been a long line at the ticket office for every showing of *The Ten Commandments*, and our matinee started at 2:00 p.m. Our minister had to stop talking before the service could end, we still had to sing another hymn, say good-bye to everybody, go home and eat lunch, then drive downtown and find a place to park, and get into line at the theater.

Dad lifted the Bible out of the pew rack and placed it in my lap with Exodus 7 open. He wanted me to read it to myself and stop being fidgety. I didn't understand all the words the Bible used, but I knew enough to be excited that a movie about Moses was sure to show the plagues God inflicted when the Egyptian pharaoh had refused to let the Israelites be free to worship God.

The first plague gave me the chills, imagining how awful it would be to see water in a river turn into blood and then wondering what died—or who died—to put that much blood in the river. The second plague of frogs might not have been too awful, except if thousands were swarming around and you squashed some underfoot trying to get away. Imagining the sound of stepping on a frog made my stomach turn over. Did they have little bones you'd hear breaking? Would that be in the movie?

In Exodus 9, God gave people boils, so they were covered with oozing, painful sores. I wondered if I'd be brave enough to help people who had boils, or if I'd be afraid of catching them and want to keep my distance. God also sent burning hail down on people, who had to run for their lives. If that happened to us, I thought, we could run into the house and listen to it falling on the roof, looking out the window to see the streaks of lightning outside. If God made it dark for three days now, longer than any eclipse, I'd worry that the sun might never return. I kept reading. In Exodus 10, the locusts swarmed onto everything like a huge, suffocating cloud. If my family faced locusts, we could hide in the basement with the doors and windows locked until they ate all the crops and flew away.

Nine plagues, and still the pharaoh didn't let the Israelites leave. I looked away from the page. I didn't want to read about the tenth plague. We'd learned in Sunday school that God finally got angry with the Egyptians *and* the Israelites and vowed to kill all their firstborn children. The Israelites had faith in God's mercy so they sacrificed lambs and spread lamb's blood on the doors of their houses, so God's avenging angels passed by the Israelites' homes and didn't kill their babies. I knew that's what the Jews still celebrate as Passover, but I didn't want to read about it. I was a firstborn child, after all.

I already knew that the Egyptian babies got killed. Grieving the loss of his own son, the pharaoh admitted that the Israelites' God was the most powerful God of all. He finally agreed to let the Israelites follow Moses out of Egypt. God parted the Red Sea to help them, then drowned the Egyptian soldiers chasing them.

I stared at the front of the church with its big cross hanging behind the organ. The minister was saying something about God's mercy. I was thinking about the Exodus. What confused me about this Bible story was why God got angry and vengeful when people didn't believe in Him. In other places in the Bible, God could be kind and loving when people were obedient. Why couldn't God be merciful to everyone all the time, even people who didn't believe in Him? We never talked about people in China or India in Sunday school. Why didn't God care about people in faraway places?

I closed the Bible on my doubts and put it back in the pew rack. I sat quietly in the pew between my parents in the familiar vaulted First Presbyterian sanctuary, sunlight streaming through the vast stained-glass windows. I wasn't listening to the sermon, only waiting for it to end so we'd be released to go to the movie. I hoped the plagues in the movie wouldn't be too scary. I wanted to see those ancient miracles happening, just not that tenth plague.

When the Sunday service *finally* ended, and we were all released, I raced out ahead of my parents to the car. At home we sat to eat a lunch Mom had already prepared.

"I grew up in Two Rivers with Charlton Heston's wife," said my dad between bites. "Her name was Lydia."

I dropped my fork. "You know Charlton Heston's wife?!"

Dad winked at Mom as he said, "Lydia Clarke was the prettiest girl in town."

Mom was unperturbed. "You've told this story before, Richard. You were a spindly high school freshman and she was a senior."

"I never heard this before," I protested. "Did you ever meet Charlton Heston?"

"She moved away to be an actress," Dad said. "She married him later."

"But he must have visited Two Rivers," I said.

Dad shrugged. "Couldn't prove it by me. I moved away too." He smiled at Mom again. "And met your beautiful mother."

Mom smiled back at him.

I was disappointed Dad had never met the movie star, but I could still claim bragging rights that my dad knew the woman who married Charlton Heston. None of my friends could say that.

Mom let me leave our dirty dishes in the sink to wash later, and we hurried to the car. We arrived at the movie theater in time to take our places on the sidewalk as the fifteenth, sixteenth, and seventeenth people in the ticket line. In 1959, the Fox Theater was the showiest movie theater in Missoula with FOX written in neon lights you could see from anywhere when it got dark. I waved to a few friends I saw in line with their families as we inched our way toward the ticket booth. Like us, everyone still wore their church clothes. I grinned in pride to be in the midst of the most exciting event in town, waiting with my pretty mom, in our matching coats, standing beside my tall, handsome dad who almost knew Charlton Heston.

Like our walk into the church, I took both my parents' hands again as we crossed the threshold out of the daylight and stepped into the theater lobby. We all stopped, our eyes needing to adjust to the low light before we walked through a curtained archway. A few older boys in trim uniforms and porkpie hats greeted people. The sound of popping kernels drew my attention to the right, where people waited in line at a concession stand to buy popcorn and soda and candy. Dad suggested we find our seats, then he'd come back to get us some treats.

The theater ceiling looked as high as the one in church. There were rows of plush red pews and an aisle down the middle. Faint light came from fancy glass globes high on the walls and from a giant chandelier overhead, shimmering with countless crystals. Paintings of teepees and animals and feathers covered the walls reflecting how Montana sat in the middle of Flathead Indian Territory.

Dad led us to a row and we apologized our way into three middle seats together. I was lightheaded with anticipation. My cheeks felt flushed. Now that the moment was here, I wanted to slow everything down so it would last forever. Dad made his way to the aisle again and out to the lobby, returning with a bag of popcorn for each of us, and a Hershey bar. A boy in my class passed by and stuck his tongue out at me, so I ignored him.

"He likes you," Mom observed.

"Does not," I said, not wanting her to know I knew and didn't mind. He had dark eyes, dark hair that fell over his forehead, and a charmer's smile—the first rogue in my life.

Mom broke the Hershey bar into three equal pieces and distributed them. I let one square melt on my tongue, savoring the sweetness and saving the rest for later.

Finally, the lights lowered until all was dark, except for a few red Exit signs. Silence reigned. The mammoth red curtains parted and a beam of light shot out from a small window in the theater's rear wall onto the screen—the movie was starting!

The first scene was a surprise, though, because the giant curtain in our theater slowly opened, to show a closed curtain over a movie screen in another movie theater. Then a bald man in a suit walked out between the movie screen curtains and walked to a microphone. Without introducing himself, he spoke at us as though he could see us. His photograph had been in *Life* magazine so I knew he was the director of the movie, Cecil B. DeMille. The movie cost $13 million, the most expensive movie ever made, I read in the article.

Mr. DeMille told us *The Ten Commandments* was the story of Moses who lived thousands of years before Jesus. Nobody knew about Moses's life, Mr. DeMille said, between the time he was three months old and discovered in a basket floating in the bulrushes, until he was 30 years old and discovered the truth that he was Hebrew, not Egyptian. Mr. DeMille said this movie was very special because of the historical research they'd done to find out what happened in those missing 30 years. He said the story of Moses was a search for freedom, a search inspired by God. Without saying good-bye, Mr. DeMille turned and went back through the on-screen movie curtain.

As the screen went black, Mr. DeMille's voice said, "And God said, 'Let there be light.'"

The movie burst onto the screen—frightening scenes of Egyptian soldiers raiding hovels, raising swords over babies in the arms of their mothers, who screamed and ran in fear. Horrified, I covered my ears and looked away from the screen, glad for the feel of my mother's arm around me, pulling me closer. I kept my head on her shoulder until the screams in the movie faded.

"Baby Moses is saved," Mom whispered, giving me the courage to watch again. Moses's mother put him in a basket on the Nile River, and an Egyptian woman found him and named the baby Moses. Nobody knew he was an Israelite, and baby Moses didn't either. As the grownup Moses, Charlton Heston, looked like an Egyptian hieroglyph come to life, as big as a god on a screen twice as wide as it was tall. He often stood still with his feet apart, the stance ancient Egyptians drew to depict people in a static pose facing to the side, like they were plastered flat on the wall. Charlton Heston wore sandals, skirts not trousers, capes with gold trim, and a regal headdress. No wonder Egyptians thought their pharaohs were gods.

I probably would have too. I was enthralled by the panoramas of ancient Egypt, the camels, the desert oases. I felt sand underfoot and wind in my hair. Every color looked more vivid than in real life.

When water in the Nile River started running red, the people in the theater—I did too—gasped to realize the water had turned into blood. This was the first punishing plague the Bible said God sent to punish Egypt.

The burning hail fell from the sky, like deadly fireworks making people scream and run in fear. In those olden times, and even in modern times, I didn't think anyone could explain how hail could burn. It would take a miracle.

I was waiting to see the plague of all the frogs hopping through the streets, and the people getting boils all over, and the locusts swarming and darkening the sky—but to my surprise, none of them got shown. The movie skipped over the other plagues but kept the worst one: killing the firstborn babies. I went cold, stared down at my lap, and put my hands over my ears, not wanting to hear the mothers' screams. I held my own mother's hand tightly. Mom leaned her head against mine and stroked my back until the danger was over. When the light in the theater changed and the music softened, I dared to open my eyes and watch the rest of the movie. When the pharaoh's own baby died, I felt awful for him, he was so devastated. He told Moses to take the Israelites and leave Egypt.

The Israelites were happy to leave. On their trip through the desert, they drank and danced late into the night, and worshipped olden gods. Moses got angry. He went up the mountain and came back with the tablets of the Ten Commandments, with God's instructions to worship only Him and how to be a good person. I was disappointed we didn't get to see God except as a blinding light. The Israelites finally listened to God's laws.

The scenes of their final escape out of Egypt kept me on the edge of my seat, my pulse pounding, even knowing the Israelites would escape because the Bible said so. Charlton Heston stood on a cliff in sandals and robe, his long hair blowing in the wind and his staff raised high overhead, imploring God. We watched a miracle as the Red Sea parted, making giant walls of water to the right and left to let the Israelites walk safely on the sea bottom across to the far side. I was glad God saved them, but regretted when He let the Egyptians get halfway across, then made the water crash in again and drown them. I was sorry God was so cruel to the Egyptians; if He'd been kinder and they'd survived, maybe some of them would have become believers.

The Red Sea and the music got calmer. So did my breath and my pulse. Moses and God had been victorious. The Israelites were free.

The End.

I sat still in the dark, my senses swirling. I didn't want the spell broken. When the theater lights came on, I didn't want to leave the theater. When I did leave with my parents, I was startled to step out into the daylight, clouds obscuring the blue sky. Walking to the car, I worried whether it might start hailing on our heads, and whether the hail would be burning.

"What did you think of the movie?" Dad asked us.

"Charlton Heston certainly is handsome," Mom said, making Dad chuckle.

"Those archers landed burning arrows on target at a hundred yards or more," said Dad with reverence, being a prize-winning archer himself.

"Look, there's a sale," Mom remarked as we passed her favorite store with sale signs in the window. "I might look for something new for the Bryson's party."

I remained silent almost all the way home.

"When people talked to God that long ago, He answered," I finally said. "Why doesn't He do that anymore?"

"He does answer prayers," Mom said, "in His own way."

She had a point. I'd prayed for a Red Flyer sled for Christmas, and Santa Claus brought me one, renewing my faith in Christmas miracles.

That night I excused myself to go to bed early, uninterested in watching *The Ed Sullivan Show*. Our black and white TV set now seemed miniscule, compared to VistaVision. I snuck a bedsheet out of the linen closet on the way to my room, then carefully closed the door and wrapped the sheet around me, like the robes women wore in ancient times. I folded my most colorful square scarf into a triangle and instead of tying it under my chin like always, tied it behind my neck and covered the knot with my hair. I threw off my shoes and walked barefoot back and forth in my room with as much slither as I could manage. This is the world I wanted to live in from now on, with movies that made me laugh and cry and dance around. That night, I dreamt of golden chariots and burning hail and flying arrows and mothers weeping.

I never saw a movie in a movie theater again with both my parents, but *The Ten Commandments* began my devotion to movies, a path that helped me define my own sensibilities and values independent of my parents' world. In the movies, I saw people face their fears and prevail, or sometimes fail tragically. People in movies knew words to express their feelings, risked everything for love or country, stood their ground even when they were all alone. Movies gave me experiences and lessons I could have gotten nowhere else.

When I left home for college, my parents soon separated, divorcing a year later. Through my own pain and confusion, movies helped me keep to my own path and hopes. "I didst give it Thee before Thou didst request it," actress Olivia Hussey as Juliet says in Franco Zeffirelli's movie *Romeo and Juliet,* Shakespeare giving her the courage to dare to offer her hand first to Romeo, played by Leonard Whiting. I yearned to have courage in love. "Stick with me, Dr. Markowitz," the charmingly shiftless Jason Robards says to Barbara Harris's earnest and nervous social worker in Herb Gardner's screenplay of his play *A Thousand Clowns.* "Anything can happen above an abandoned Chinese restaurant." I yearned to have the courage of defiance and humor even in dire circumstances.

Yet no movie scene about love is more vivid to me than the real life memory of holding both my parents' hands as we walked together into the movie theater to see *The Ten Commandments*. Even if love eventually ends, I know its memory always matters.

Jennifer Wilke has been a newspaper columnist and playwright, an educational TV scriptwriter, and an aspiring screenwriter in Los Angeles. She has recently completed her first historical novel, *The Color of Prayer*. This anthology piece is from her developing memoir, *After a Little Rain on Thursday*.

CPSIA information can be obtained
at www.ICGtesting.com
Printed in the USA
FFHW022331070219
50437523-55632FF